15th Workshop on Building and Using Comparable Corpora (BUCC 2022)

AA005124

Held at LREC 2022

Marseille, France
25 June 2022

Editors:

Reinhard Rapp
Pierre Zweigenbaum
Serge Sharoff

ISBN: 978-1-7138-6113-3

Printed from e-media with permission by:

Curran Associates, Inc.
57 Morehouse Lane
Red Hook, NY 12571

Some format issues inherent in the e-media version may also appear in this print version.

Copyright© (2022) by the Association for Computational Linguistics
All rights reserved.
Copyright for individual papers remains with the authors and are licensed under a Creative Commons 4.0 license, CC-BY-ND. (https://creativecommons.org/licenses/by-nd/4.0/)

Printed with permission by Curran Associates, Inc. (2022)

For permission requests, please contact the Association for Computational Linguistics at the address below.

Association for Computational Linguistics
209 N. Eighth Street
Stroudsburg, Pennsylvania 18360

Phone: 1-570-476-8006
Fax: 1-570-476-0860

acl@aclweb.org

Additional copies of this publication are available from:

Curran Associates, Inc.
57 Morehouse Lane
Red Hook, NY 12571 USA
Phone: 845-758-0400
Fax: 845-758-2633
Email: curran@proceedings.com
Web: www.proceedings.com

LREC 2022 Workshop
Language Resources and Evaluation Conference
25 June 2022

15th Workshop on Building and Using Comparable Corpora
(BUCC 2022)

PROCEEDINGS

Editors:
Reinhard Rapp, Pierre Zweigenbaum, Serge Sharoff

Proceedings of the LREC 2022
15th Workshop on Building and Using Comparable Corpora
(BUCC 2022)

Edited by:
Reinhard Rapp, Pierre Zweigenbaum, Serge Sharoff

For more information:
European Language Resources Association (ELRA)
9 rue des Cordelières
75013, Paris
France
http://www.elra.info
Email: lrec@elda.org

© European Language Resources Association (ELRA)

These workshop proceedings are licensed under a Creative Commons
Attribution-NonCommercial 4.0 International License

Preface – 15th BUCC at LREC 2022)

This volume documents the Proceedings of the 15th Workshop on Building and Using Comparable Corpora, held on June 25, 2022, as part of the LREC 2022 conference (International Conference on Language Resources and Evaluation).

In the language engineering and the linguistics communities, research on comparable corpora has been motivated by two main reasons. In language engineering, on the one hand, it is primarily motivated by the need to use comparable corpora as training data for statistical Natural Language Processing applications such as statistical machine translation or cross-lingual retrieval. In linguistics, on the other hand, comparable corpora are of interest in themselves by making possible inter-linguistic discoveries and comparisons. It is generally accepted in both communities that comparable corpora are documents in one or several languages that are comparable in content and form in various degrees and dimensions. We believe that the linguistic definitions and observations related to comparable corpora can improve methods to mine such corpora for applications of statistical NLP. As such, it is of great interest to bring together builders and users of such corpora.

Comparable corpora are collections of documents that are comparable in content and form in various degrees and dimensions. This definition includes many types of parallel and non-parallel multilingual corpora, but also sets of monolingual corpora that are used for comparative purposes. Research on comparable corpora is active but used to be scattered among many workshops and conferences. The workshop series on "Building and Using Comparable Corpora" (BUCC) aims at promoting progress in this exciting field by bundling its research, thereby making it more visible and giving it a better platform.

The first 12 of the 14 previous editions of the workshop took place in Africa (LREC'08 in Marrakech), America (ACL'11 in Portland and ACL'17 in Vancouver), Asia (ACL-IJCNLP'09 in Singapore, ACL-IJCNLP'15 in Beijing, LREC'18 in Miyazaki, Japan), Europe (LREC'10 in Malta, ACL'13 in Sofia, LREC'14 in Reykjavik, LREC'16 in Portoroz, RANLP'19 in Varna) and also on the border between Asia and Europe (LREC'12 in Istanbul). Due to the Corona crises, in the past two years the conference was held online in conjunction with LREC'20 and with RANLP'21.

Part of this year's edition of the BUCC workshop was a shared task on "Bilingual Term Alignment in Comparable Specialized Corpora" which is documented in these proceedings..

We would like to thank all people who in one way or another helped in making this workshop once again a success. We are especially grateful to Khalid Choukri for his extraordinary guidance concerning the proceedings, to Nicoletta Calzolari for her continuous support of our workshop, and to Hélène Mazo, Sara Goggi and the whole team of LREC organisers for finding solutions to all matters of concern.

Our special thanks go to our invited speakers and to the members of the programme committee who did an excellent job in reviewing the submitted papers under strict time constraints. Last but not least we would like to thank our authors, shared task teams and all participants of the workshop.

Reinhard Rapp, Pierre Zweigenbaum, Serge Sharoff June 2022

Workshop Organizers

Reinhard Rapp, Athena R.C., Magdeburg-Stendal University of Applied Sciences, University of Mainz (workshop chair)
Pierre Zweigenbaum, Université Paris-Saclay, CNRS, LISN (shared task chair)
Serge Sharoff, University of Leeds

Programme Committee

Ahmet Aker (University of Sheffield, UK)
Ebrahim Ansari (Institute for Advanced Studies in Basic Sciences, Iran)
Thierry Etchegoyhen (VicomTech, Spain)
Hitoshi Isahara (Otemon Gakuin University, Japan)
Kyo Kageura (The University of Tokyo, Japan)
Natalie Kübler (Université de Paris, France)
Philippe Langlais (Université de Montréal, Canada)
Yves Lepage (Waseda University, Japan)
Michael Mohler (Language Computer Corp., USA)
Emmanuel Morin (Université de Nantes, France)
Dragos Stefan Munteanu (Language Weaver, Inc., USA)
Ted Pedersen (University of Minnesota, Duluth, USA)
Reinhard Rapp (Athena R.C., Greece, Magdeburg-Stendal University of Applied Sciences, University of Mainz, Germany)
Nasredine Semmar (CEA LIST, Paris, France)
Serge Sharoff (University of Leeds, UK)
Michel Simard (National Research Council Canada)
Richard Sproat (OGI School of Science & Technology, USA)
Pierre Zweigenbaum (Université Paris-Saclay, CNRS, LISN, Orsay, France)

Table of Contents

Workshop Programme

09:00–9:05 ***Opening***

Session 1: Invited Presentation

09:05–10:00

Session 2: Comparative dependency parsing

10:00–10:30 *Multilingual Comparative Analysis of Deep-Learning Dependency Parsing Results Using Parallel Corpora*
Diego Alves, Marko Tadić and Božo Bekavac

10:30–11:00 ***Coffee Break***

Session 3: Building corpora and lexicon induction

11:00–11:30 *Building Domain-specific Corpora from the Web: the Case of European Digital Service Infrastructures*
Rik van Noord, Cristian García-Romero, Miquel Esplà-Gomis, Leopoldo Pla Sempere and Antonio Toral

11:30–12:00 *Challenges of Building Domain-Specific Parallel Corpora from Public Administration Documents*
Filip Klubička, Lorena Kasunić, Danijel Blazsetin and Petra Bago

12:00–12:30 *Setting Up Bilingual Comparable Corpora with Non-Contemporary Languages*
Helena Bermudez Sabel, Francesca Dell'Oro, Cyrielle Montrichard and Corinne Rossari

12:30–13:00 *About Evaluating Bilingual Lexicon Induction*
Martin Laville, Emmanuel Morin and Phillippe Langlais

13:00–14:00 ***Lunch Break***

Session 4: Word embeddings

14:00–14:30 *Evaluating Monolingual and Crosslingual Embeddings on Datasets of Word Association Norms*
Trina Kwong, Emmanuele Chersoni and Rong Xiang

14:30–15:00 *Don't Forget Cheap Training Signals Before Building Unsupervised Bilingual Word Embeddings*
Silvia Severini, Viktor Hangya, Masoud Jalili Sabet, Alexander Fraser and Hinrich Schütze

Session 5: Shared task on bilingual term alignment

15:00–15:30 *CUNI Submission to the BUCC 2022 Shared Task on Bilingual Term Alignment*
Borek Požár, Klára Tauchmanová, Kristýna Neumannová, Ivana Kvapilíková and Ondřej Bojar

15:30–16:00 *Fusion of linguistic, neural and sentence-transformer features for improved term alignment*
Andraz Repar, Senja Pollak, Matej Ulčar and Boshko Koloski

Workshop Programme (continued)

16:00–16:30 ***Coffee Break***

16:30–17:00 *Overview on the shared task*
Pierre Zweigenbaum

17:00–17:10 ***Closing***

Proceedings of the 15th Workshop on Building and Using Comparable Corpora (BUCC 2022) @LREC2022 , pages 1–7
Marseille, June 25, 2022
© European Language Resources Association (ELRA), licensed under CC-BY-NC

Evaluating Monolingual and Crosslingual Embeddings on Datasets of Word Association Norms

Trina Kwong[1], Emmanuele Chersoni[2], Rong Xiang[2]
King George V School[1], The Hong Kong Polytechnic University[2]
King George V School, Ho Man Tin, Kowloon, Hong Kong [1]
The Hong Kong Polytechnic University, Yuk Choi Road 11, Hung Hom, Kowloon, Hong Kong [2]
{trinakwong,emmanuelechersoni,xiangrong0302}@gmail.com

Abstract

In *free word association* tasks, human subjects are presented with a stimulus word and are then asked to name the first word (the response word) that comes up to their mind. Those associations, presumably learned on the basis of conceptual contiguity or similarity, have attracted for a long time the attention of researchers in linguistics and cognitive psychology, since they are considered as clues about the internal organization of the lexical knowledge in the semantic memory.
Word associations data have also been used to assess the performance of Vector Space Models for English, but evaluations for other languages have been relatively rare so far. In this paper, we introduce word associations datasets for Italian, Spanish and Mandarin Chinese by extracting data from the Small World of Words project, and we propose two different tasks inspired by the previous literature. We tested both monolingual and crosslingual word embeddings on the new datasets, showing that they perform similarly in the evaluation tasks.

Keywords: Word Associations, Distributional Semantic Models, Crosslingual Embeddings

1. Introduction

With the expression "semantic memory", linguists and psychologists tend to refer to the people's memory for conceptual and linguistic meanings, and the way in which this knowledge is encoded and organized has always been a common point of interest. A commonly used metaphor is that of a network, where nodes represent words and the lines linking them are the connections between those words (Fitzpatrick, 2012). When it comes to the specific problem of the organization of word meanings, the procedure known as *word association norms* is probably the most typical mean of investigation: a stimulus word is presented to a human participant, who is simply required to produce the first word coming to mind (McRae et al., 2012). Most authors agree that word associations are learned by contiguity (Church and Hanks, 1990; Wettler et al., 2005; Rapp, 2014), and that they play a fundamental role in language learning (McRae et al., 2012). Some of the modern theories of linguistic and conceptual processing even assume that they capture most of the semantic representations in the language system (Barsalou et al., 2008; De Deyne and Storms, 2008).

One of the strongest paradigm in computational semantics research, on the other hand, has been focusing on the representation of words as distributional vectors, and on the assessment of their semantic similarity on the basis of the similarity of the linguistic patterns of co-occurrence, extracted from large scale textual corpora (Turney and Pantel, 2010; Lenci, 2018). Given the success of *Vector Space Models* (henceforth VSMs) such as Word2Vec (Mikolov et al., 2013) and GloVe (Pennington et al., 2014), researchers in cognitive science successfully tested them on a variety of psycholinguistic tasks, including the prediction of word associates (Mandera et al., 2017; Nematzadeh et al., 2017), the modeling of human-elicited cloze completion of sentences (Hofmann et al., 2017) and of association ratings (Hofmann et al., 2018). Interestingly, VSMs that are trained directly on word associations have been shown to outperform those trained on textual corpora in predicting human similarity and relatedness judgements, suggesting that such associations are providing a more accurate reflection of the structure of the mental lexicon (De Deyne et al., 2016). Although new benchmarks for modeling word associations with VSMs have recently been introduced (Evert and Lapesa, 2021), however, this kind of evaluation task has almost always been done in English, also because of the lack of similar word association datasets for other languages.

In this paper, we describe the creation of three comparable word association datasets for Italian, Spanish and Mandarin Chinese, which were manually compiled by extracting the data from the interface of the website of the Small World of Words project (De Deyne et al., 2019), and we propose a first evaluation with word embedding models. [1] In addition to monolingual word embeddings for each language, we also used *crosslingual embeddings* (Ruder et al., 2019) that represent the lexicon of two or more languages in the same semantic space. Our results show some differences between languages, but in general the crosslingual embeddings perform comparably to monolingual ones. [2]

[1] https://smallworldofwords.org/en/project/explore

[2] The datasets described in this work will be available upon publication. For more information, contact emmanuelechersoni@gmail.com.

2. Related Work

2.1. Free Association Data for VSMs Evaluation

Using free association data, two types of evaluation tasks can be designed: in the *forward association* task, a model is given a stimulus word and it has to produce the first associate (*lucky* → ? *fox* → ?), while in the *backward* or *reverse* association task the model is presented with one or more response words, and it has to identify the originary stimulus (for example, it would have to guess that *cloud, pizza, drug, kingdom* and *chewy* are responses to the stimulus *mushroom*). The evaluation in the first type of task is typically challenging, since there is a high amount of variation in word production (Rapp, 2008; Rapp, 2014) and the model would have to pick the right answer out of thousands of possible alternatives (Evert and Lapesa, 2021). Some tasks based on the forward associations of the Edinburgh Associative Thesaurus (Kiss et al., 1973) were introduced first in the ESSLLI 2008 Workshop on Lexical Semantics (Baroni et al., 2008). Among the others, the authors proposed a multiple choice discrimination task: given tuples composed by a cue word, a first associate, a hapax associate (e.g. a response produced only once for a given stimulus) and a random associate, a VSM had to assign a higher similarity score to the cue-first pair. They also introduced the more challenging open-vocabulary access task where, for each cue word, a VSM had to retrieve the first associate from an open set of possible response words.

More recently, a much larger free associations dataset for word embeddings evaluation in English has been created by Evert and Lapesa (2021), with more than 12000 association tuples extracted from the Edinburgh Associative Thesaurus and from the Southern Florida Association Norms (Nelson et al., 2004). Evert and Lapesa proposed a multiple choice task and an open vocabulary access task, similarly to Baroni et al. (2008), and reported that in the former the best performance is obtained by first-order models, based on collocations, while VSMs do better in the latter one. The two types of models seemed to have complementary strengths since their combination further improved the global accuracy scores.

As for *reverse associations*, a task example was instead proposed by Rapp (2014): given a list of response words, a system has to predict the stimulus word leading to their production. Reverse association can be also seen as related to lexical access issues, such as the so-called *tip-of-the-tongue* problem, when a person cannot recall a particular word but can still think to its features and associates (Zock and Bilac, 2004; Zock et al., 2010; Zock and Schwab, 2011). Moreover, as suggested by Zock (2002), an automatic tool that is able to efficiently retrieve a target word from its associates could be potentially very useful for navigating lexical resources. Following Rapp's proposal, the CogALex Shared Task 2014 (Rapp and Zock, 2014) introduced an evaluation dataset of responses and stimuli, also based on the Edinburgh Associative Thesaurus. The best results were reported by Ghosh et al. (2014), who used vector similarities from a Word2Vec vector space (Mikolov et al., 2013) to generate cue candidates and then ranked them on the basis of Pointwise Mutual Information scores (Church and Hanks, 1990).

2.2. Predicting Norms with Word Embeddings

A common criticism of VSMs is that, as a semantic representation, they are not grounded in perception and word meanings are only defined in relation to each other (Glenberg and Robertson, 2000; Fagarasan et al., 2015). Several works, for this reason, proposed to map word embedding features onto interpretable norms of different types via regression or neural network methods, e.g. conceptual (Fagarasan et al., 2015; Li and Summers-Stay, 2019), modality exclusivity (Chersoni et al., 2020) or neurocognitive norms (Utsumi, 2018; Utsumi, 2020; Chersoni et al., 2021).

Chersoni et al. (2020) recently reported that norms for a new language can be decently predicted with a machine learning classifier trained on English norms and *crosslingual word embeddings*, a kind of VSM that represents the lexicon of two or more languages in the same semantic space. This kind of crosslingual prediction could be an interesting application for psycholinguistic research relying on norms, as norms are generally available only for a few languages other than English and their collection is typically time-consuming. Being able to automatically predict norms for under-resourced languages via crosslingual transfer, on the other hand, would certainly represent a big advantage.

In our work, we decided to test also crosslingual word embeddings in word association tasks, to assess to what extent word association knowledge can be modeled with multilingual semantic spaces. According to some previous studies (Brainerd et al., 2008; McRae et al., 2012), word associations are to be understood in terms of semantic relations, and those relations could be at least partially shared across languages. However, it should also be considered that responses to a cue might depend on language-specific patterns, and such cases are expected to be more challenging for models aligning multiple languages in the same semantic space. [3]

3. Experimental Settings

3.1. Dataset Creation

For the Italian, Spanish and Mandarin Chinese datasets, we manually collected word associations data by querying the `https://smallworldofwords.org/en/project/explore`, as it contains data for many different languages and words that are filtered by a minimum frequency threshold. Each dataset includes 300 stimuli words. At the beginning, we tried

[3] In this work, the expressions *Vector Space Models* (VSMs) and *word embeddings* are used interchangeably.

to select the 300 words of the original ESSLLI 2008 dataset (Baroni et al., 2008) and to translate them in the other languages; however, we found out that the coverage was low, i.e. different stimuli have been used for different languages. Therefore, we just selected the stimuli for each language by using the random selection function of the project interface. It should also be noticed that the Small World of Words is an ongoing project, and new data gets continuously added: the datasets described here refer to the status of the collection as of December 2021.

For each stimulus, we generated a tuple of words <FIRST HIGHER RANDOM>, where:

- FIRST is the first associate word, the one that was produced more frequently as a response to a stimulus word;
- HIGHER is a higher-rank associate word, i.e. a word that is not the first but the n-th in a rank based on the decreasing number of subjects that produced it as a response. This word will still be related to the stimulus, but is likely to reflect a weaker association strength. For all datasets, we always sampled HIGHER words with the minimum frequency that was available on the Small World of Words website for the given stimulus, i.e. 2 for most words, meaning that all those words have been produced by at least 2 subjects;
- RANDOM was a word that was randomly picked out of the pool of the first associates of the other stimuli in the same language. The sampling was carried out by using the Python RANDOM package, and the same word could have been sampled multiple times.

Examples of the generated tuples for each language can be seen in Table 1.

The words in the Small World of Words interface are not lemmatized, and therefore the frequencies are split over morphologically-related forms. For our datasets, we considered the unlemmatized forms, that is, the frequencies were kept separate for different morphological forms of the same word.

Finally, for each tuple we added an association score between the stimulus and the FIRST associate, to be used for extra analysis. Following Baroni et al. (2008), this score was computed by taking the number of the responses for the FIRST associate of a given stimulus and dividing it by the total number of responses for that stimulus. For example, if a FIRST associate has been produced 5 times out of 10 responses, the association score for the tuple will be 0.5. This score could be eventually used to design other evaluation tasks, for example by assessing the correlation between the association and similarity scores produced by a word embedding model.

A noticeable difference between our datasets and the previous ones is represented by the HIGHER associates. In the works by Baroni et al. (2008) and Evert and Lapesa (2021), the tuples contained HAPAX associates, i.e. words that were produced only once as a response to the stimulus. However, the Small World of Words website does not include such responses, as the minimum frequency is 2. Evert and Lapesa (2021) used the HAPAX associates as distractors, in order to make the task more challenging for VSMs. Since our HIGHER associates have been produced more than one subjects, we expected them to have a higher association strength with the original stimulus, and thus, to be more difficult to discriminate from the FIRST associates.

Lang	Stimulus	First	Higher	Random
ITA	linea (line)	retta (straight)	lunga (long)	prete (priest)
SPA	bueno (good)	malo (bad)	dulce (sweet)	verde (green)
ZH	活 (live)	死 (die)	人生 (life)	人才 (talent, talented person)

Table 1: Examples of the tuples for each language

Model	Corpus	Type
FastText Wiki	Wikipedia	Monolingual
FastText WikiAlign	Wikipedia	Crosslingual (2 languages)
Numberbatch	ConceptNet, Word2Vec, Glove OpenSubtitles 2016	Multilingual (78 languages)

Table 2: Summary of word embedding types.

3.2. VSMs

For each language, we used three 300-dimensional off-the-shelf word embedding models, which are summarized in Table 2. One of them is a monolingual model, i.e. the publicly available FastText vectors (Bojanowski et al., 2017; Grave et al., 2018) trained with a Skip Gram model on Wikipedia (*FastText Wiki*). [4], [5]

Together with the monolingual *FastText Wiki* vectors, we also tested the crosslingual vectors of *FastText WikiAlign* (Joulin et al., 2018). In the *FastText WikiAlign* models [6], the embeddings of English a source language have been aligned to the embeddings of a target language, using a mapping function that minimizes the distances between words that are reciprocal translations, and maximizes the margin between correct translations and other candidate words.

Finally, we also experimented with the multilingual *Numberbatch* embeddings (Speer and Lowry-Duda, 2017), which are obtained by retrofitting different types of word embeddings with a subgraph of ConceptNet (Speer et al., 2017). We used the more recent release

[4]https://fasttext.cc/docs/en/pretrained-vectors.html

[5]All the hyperparameters are the default ones of the Word2Vec package, see Mikolov et al. (2013) for details.

[6]https://fasttext.cc/docs/en/aligned-vectors.html

of Numberbatch, where the sources of the retrofitted embeddings are Word2Vec, GloVe and the OpenSubtitles2016 corpus (Lison and Tiedemann, 2016).

3.3. Tasks and Metrics

For the evaluation tasks, we follow the design of the two tasks proposed by the previous literature (Baroni et al., 2008; Evert and Lapesa, 2021). In the **multiple choice task**, given a stimulus and a tuple <FIRST HIGHER RANDOM>, the word embedding model should be able to determine which one of the words in the tuple is the FIRST associate. For each embedding space, we simply compute the cosine similarity of the stimulus vector and the vectors of the three words in the tuple, and assign a hit whenever the similarity score with the FIRST word is the highest. Performance is assessed using the standard *Accuracy* metric.

In the **open-vocabulary access task**, for each stimulus in the dataset, a word embedding model has to retrieve the right FIRST associate out of a list of candidates including all the other FIRST associates in the dataset (e.g. for each language, there will be around 300 candidates). For each stimulus, we measure the cosine similarity with all the other FIRST associates in the dataset and we compile a ranking based on decreasing similarity values. We then assess the performance with the following metrics:

- *Top-N Accuracy*: we assign a hit whenever the right FIRST associate for a stimulus is in the top-N of the rank. We reported Accuracy values for $N = 1, 5, 10$;
- *Mean Rank*: we compute the average rank of the right FIRST associate for each stimulus (see Equation 1). For $rank_i$, we use directly the index of instance i if the right FIRST associate is in the top 10 of the rank, and 10 otherwise.

$$MeanRank = \frac{1}{n} * \sum_{i=1}^{n} rank_i \qquad (1)$$

Notice that for the latter metric, the lower the score the better, as we want a model to push the right FIRST associates at rank 1 (or as close as possible).

4. Results and Analysis

Table 3 reports the scores for the Multiple Choice Task in the three target languages. The models have full or almost full coverage for the Spanish and Italian dataset, while the Wikipedia-based models for Chinese have several missing words.

For the two European languages, it can be noticed that Wikipedia-based models are the better performing ones, with the monolingual and the crosslingual model achieving similar accuracy scores. As for the Chinese dataset, the situation is reversed: Numberbatch is the model achieving the highest Accuracy scores, and it also shows a better coverage of the dataset vocabulary.

The scores might not seem particularly high, especially in comparison with previous evaluation of this task on English data (Evert and Lapesa, 2021), but besides the limit of our evaluation (e.g. we are also testing VSMs, but no first-order models based on collocations), it should also be considered that our HIGHER distractors are likely to be much more difficult to disentangle from FIRST associates than the HAPAX words of the previous datasets. The reason is that the HAPAX words were associates being produced only by one subject in response to a stimulus, while our HIGHER associates have been produced by two or more subjects, and thus they are likely to reflect less sporadic associations in the mental lexicon. A partial proof of this can be seen in Table 4, 5 and 6, which report, for each dataset, the number of highest cosine scores per condition. At a glance, it is clear that for all models the stimulus-FIRST pair has the highest number of highest cosine scores, but HIGHER words are efficient distractors, leading to a consistent number of errors.

To assess how good the models are at discriminating between the three conditions, we also ran a Kruskal-Wallis test by means of the the R statistical software.The scores for all models show significant differences by condition ($p < 0.001$). We then ran Wilcoxon tests with Bonferroni correction for the pairwise comparisons, and we found strongly significant differences ($p < 0.001$) for almost all of them, with just a small exception, i.e. a weaker effect ($p < 0.05$) for FastText-Wiki for Chinese.

The results of the Open-Vocabulary Access Task for each language can be seen in Tables 7, 8 and 9. They follow similar patterns: for Italian and Spanish, FastText-Wiki and FastText-WikiAlign are the best models in terms of Top1-Accuracy and MeanRank, with the Numberbatch model clearly lagging behind. It should also be mentioned that the Numberbatch model has generally low scores for Top-1 Accuracy, but on the other hand is quite consistent across languages in retrieving the FIRST candidate in the first 5-10 rank positions, and thus its scores for MeanRank, Top-5 and Top-10 Accuracy are closer to the other models.

As for Chinese, Numberbatch is the best model for all metrics, except for the Top-1 Accuracy, where it is topped by FastText WikiAlign. Interestingly, both crosslingual models achieve higher scores on the Chinese data.

A general observation can be made: the crosslingual embeddings are always competitive with the monolingual ones, or even slightly better. In Task 1, FastText-WikiAlign even achieves the top score for Spanish, and in Task 2 the crosslingual models outperform the monolingual models for all metrics on Italian and Spanish. Chinese was expected to be more difficult, as it is a more typologically distant language from English than Spanish and Italian are. However, the Numberbatch embeddings still do better than the monolingual model in all metrics.

Task 1	Italian		Spanish		Chinese	
	Accuracy	Missing Words/ Vocab Size	Accuracy	Missing Words/ Vocab Size	Accuracy	Missing Words/ Vocab Size
FastText-Wiki	**0.723**	0/718	0.657	1/789	0.590	65/809
FastText-WikiAlign	0.717	0/718	**0.673**	1/789	0.630	65/809
Numberbatch	0.623	0/718	0.647	2/789	**0.670**	23/809

Table 3: Results for the Multiple Choice Task in terms of Accuracy for all languages (the top scores are **in bold**). Missing words and vocabulary size are also reported.

	FIRST	HIGHER	RANDOM
FastText-Wiki	216	82	2
FastText-WikiAlign	214	83	3
Numberbatch	187	88	25

Table 4: Number of highest similarity scores with the stimulus in Task 1 for Italian.

	FIRST	HIGHER	RANDOM
FastText-Wiki	193	94	13
FastText-WikiAlign	198	88	14
Numberbatch	194	88	18

Table 5: Number of highest similarity scores with the stimulus in Task 1 for Spanish.

	FIRST	HIGHER	RANDOM
FastText-Wiki	177	97	26
FastText-WikiAlign	189	90	21
Numberbatch	201	95	4

Table 6: Number of highest similarity scores with the stimulus in Task 1 for Chinese.

Task2-Italian	Acc1	Acc5	Acc10	Mean Rank
FastText-Wiki	0.257	**0.533**	**0.630**	5.577
FastText-WikiAlign	**0.263**	**0.533**	**0.630**	**5.523**
Numberbatch	0.120	0.423	0.520	6.580

Table 7: Results for the open-vocabulary task for Italian. Top-N Accuracy for $N = 1, 5, 10$ and Mean Rank are reported (for the latter metric, the lower the better).

Task2-Spanish	Acc1	Acc5	Acc10	Mean Rank
FastText-Wiki	0.268	0.482	0.572	5.823
FastText-WikiAlign	**0.281**	**0.528**	**0.609**	**5.569**
Numberbatch	0.144	0.475	0.548	6.204

Table 8: Results for the open-vocabulary task for Spanish. Top-N Accuracy for $N = 1, 5, 10$ and Mean Rank are reported (for the latter metric, the lower the better).

Also because of the small size of the datasets, the performance differences between models are not significantly different. However, we still think our results can be taken as preliminary evidence that the alignment of embeddings in multilingual spaces does not detract too much from their ability of modeling word associations data in the target language.

Task2-Chinese	Acc1	Acc5	Acc10	Mean Rank
FastText-Wiki	0.170	0.253	0.317	7.757
FastText-WikiAlign	**0.203**	0.347	0.413	7.050
Numberbatch	0.183	**0.537**	**0.617**	**5.657**

Table 9: Results for the open-vocabulary task for Mandarin Chinese. Top-N Accuracy for $N = 1, 5, 10$ and Mean Rank are reported (for the latter metric, the lower the better).

5. Conclusions

In this paper, we have presented an evaluation of Vector Space Models on word associations tasks for languages other than English, after generating three new datasets for Italian, Spanish and Mandarin Chinese from the association data of the Small World of Words project.

Inspired by the previous literature, we tested Vector Space Models on a multiple choice task and on the more challenging open-vocabulary access task. We have included both monolingual and crosslingual embeddings in the evaluation, and we observed that they perform comparably, and in many settings the crosslingual model even do slightly better than their monolingual competitors. We plan to release the three datasets upon publication, in order to encourage further research on the topic.

Our finding might have interesting future applications, such as the automatic prediction of norms for other languages, using multilingual embedding spaces and/or supervised training based on data from high-resource languages (Chersoni et al., 2020). Another necessary step will be to increase the size of the data collections and to include more new languages in the word association evaluation.

Acknowledgements

The current project was carried out during Trina Kwong's internship at the Hong Kong Polytechnic University, under the program "Linguistic Training and Internship for Gifted Students" (PJTD).

The authors would like to thank Simon De Deyne for the availability to share the data extracted from the Small World of Words project.

6. Bibliographical References

Baroni, M., Evert, S., and Lenci, A. (2008). Lexical Semantics: Bridging the Gap between Semantic Theory and Computational Simulation. In *Proceedings of the ESSLLI Workshop on Distributional Lexical Semantics*.

Barsalou, L. W., Santos, A., Simmons, W. K., and Wilson, C. D. (2008). Language and Simulation in Conceptual Processing. *Symbols, Embodiment, and Meaning*, pages 245–283.

Bojanowski, P., Grave, E., Joulin, A., and Mikolov, T. (2017). Enriching Word Vectors with Subword Information. *Transactions of the Association for Computational Linguistics*, 5:135–146.

Brainerd, C. J., Yang, Y., Reyna, V. F., Howe, M. L., and Mills, B. A. (2008). Semantic Processing in "Associative" False Memory. *Psychonomic Bulletin & Review*, 15(6):1035–1053.

Chersoni, E., Xiang, R., Lu, Q., and Huang, C.-R. (2020). Automatic Learning of Modality Exclusivity Norms with Crosslingual Word Embeddings. In *Proceedings of *SEM*.

Chersoni, E., Santus, E., Huang, C.-R., and Lenci, A. (2021). Decoding Word Embeddings with Brain-Based Semantic Features. *Computational Linguistics*, 47(3):663–698.

Church, K. W. and Hanks, P. (1990). Word Association Norms, Mutual Information, and Lexicography. *Computational Linguistics*, 16(1):22–29.

De Deyne, S. and Storms, G. (2008). Word Associations: Network and Semantic Properties. *Behavior Research Methods*, 40(1):213–231.

De Deyne, S., Perfors, A., and Navarro, D. J. (2016). Predicting Human Similarity Judgments with Distributional Models: The Value of Word Associations. In *Proceedings of COLING*.

De Deyne, S., Navarro, D. J., Perfors, A., Brysbaert, M., and Storms, G. (2019). The "Small World of Words" English Word Association Norms for over 12,000 Cue Words. *Behavior Research Methods*, 51(3):987–1006.

Evert, S. and Lapesa, G. (2021). FAST: A Carefully Sampled and Cognitively Motivated Dataset for Distributional Semantic Evaluation. In *Proceedings of CONLL*.

Fagarasan, L., Vecchi, E. M., and Clark, S. (2015). From Distributional Semantics to Feature Norms: Grounding Semantic Models in Human Perceptual Data. In *Proceedings of IWCS*.

Fitzpatrick, T. (2012). Word Associations. *The Encyclopedia of Applied Linguistics*.

Ghosh, U., Jain, S., and Paul, S. (2014). A Two-stage Approach for Computing Associative Responses to a Set of Stimulus Words. In *Proceedings of the COLING Workshop on Cognitive Aspects of the Lexicon (CogALex)*.

Glenberg, A. M. and Robertson, D. A. (2000). Symbol Grounding and Meaning: A Comparison of High-Dimensional and Embodied Theories of Meaning. *Journal of Memory and Language*, 43(3):379–401.

Grave, E., Bojanowski, P., Gupta, P., Joulin, A., and Mikolov, T. (2018). Learning Word Vectors for 157 Languages. In *Proceedings of LREC*.

Hofmann, M. J., Biemann, C., and Remus, S. (2017). Benchmarking N-Grams, Topic Models and Recurrent Neural Networks by Cloze Completions, EEGs and Eye Movements. In *Cognitive Approach to Natural Language Processing*, pages 197–215. Elsevier.

Hofmann, M. J., Biemann, C., Westbury, C., Murusidze, M., Conrad, M., and Jacobs, A. M. (2018). Simple Co-Occurrence Statistics Reproducibly Predict Association Ratings. *Cognitive Science*, 42(7):2287–2312.

Joulin, A., Bojanowski, P., Mikolov, T., Jégou, H., and Grave, E. (2018). Loss in Translation: Learning Bilingual Word Mapping with a Retrieval Criterion. In *Proceedings of EMNLP*.

Kiss, G., Armstrong, C., Milroy, R., and Piper, J. R. I. (1973). An Associative Thesaurus of English and Its Computer Analysis. pages 153–165. Edinburgh University Press.

Lenci, A. (2018). Distributional Models of Word Meaning. *Annual Review of Linguistics*, 4:151–171.

Li, D. and Summers-Stay, D. (2019). Mapping Distributional Semantics to Property Norms with Deep Neural Networks. *Big Data and Cognitive Computing*, 3(2):30.

Lison, P. and Tiedemann, J. (2016). OpenSubtitles2016: Extracting Large Parallel Corpora from Movie and TV Subtitles. In *Proceedings of LREC*.

Mandera, P., Keuleers, E., and Brysbaert, M. (2017). Explaining Human Performance in Psycholinguistic Tasks with Models of Semantic Similarity Based on Prediction and Counting: A Review and Empirical Validation. *Journal of Memory and Language*, 92:57–78.

McRae, K., Khalkhali, S., and Hare, M. (2012). Semantic and Associative Relations in Adolescents and Young Adults: Examining a Tenuous Dichotomy. *Psychology Publications*, 115.

Mikolov, T., Chen, K., Corrado, G., and Dean, J. (2013). Efficient Estimation of Word Representations in Vector Space. *arXiv preprint arXiv:1301.3781*.

Nelson, D. L., McEvoy, C. L., and Schreiber, T. A. (2004). The University of South Florida Free Association, Rhyme, and Word Fragment Norms. *Behavior Research Methods, Instruments, & Computers*, 36(3):402–407.

Nematzadeh, A., Meylan, S. C., and Griffiths, T. L. (2017). Evaluating Vector-Space Models of Word Representation, or, the Unreasonable Effectiveness of Counting Words Near Other Words. In *Proceedings of CogSci*.

Pennington, J., Socher, R., and Manning, C. (2014).

Glove: Global Vectors for Word Representation. In *Proceedings of EMNLP*.

Rapp, R. and Zock, M. (2014). The CogALex-IV Shared Task on the Lexical Access Problem. In *Proceedings of the COLING Workshop on Cognitive Aspects of the Lexicon*.

Rapp, R. (2008). The Computation of Associative Responses to Multiword Stimuli. In *Proceedings of the COLING Workshop on Cognitive Aspects of the Lexicon*.

Rapp, R. (2014). Corpus-Based Computation of Reverse Associations. In *Proceedings of LREC*.

Ruder, S., Vulić, I., and Søgaard, A. (2019). A Survey of Cross-lingual Word Embedding Models. *Journal of Artificial Intelligence Research*, 65:569–631.

Speer, R. and Lowry-Duda, J. (2017). ConceptNet at SemEval-2017 Task 2: Extending Word Embeddings with Multilingual Relational Knowledge. In *Proceedings of SemEval*.

Speer, R., Chin, J., and Havasi, C. (2017). Conceptnet 5.5: An Open Multilingual Graph of General Knowledge. In *Proceedings of AAAI*.

Turney, P. D. and Pantel, P. (2010). From Frequency to Meaning: Vector Space Models of Semantics. *Journal of Artificial Intelligence Research*, 37:141–188.

Utsumi, A. (2018). A Neurobiologically Motivated Analysis of Distributional Semantic Models. In *Proceedings of CogSci*.

Utsumi, A. (2020). Exploring What Is Encoded in Distributional Word Vectors: A Neurobiologically Motivated Analysis. *Cognitive Science*, 44(6):e12844.

Wettler, M., Rapp, R., and Sedlmeier, P. (2005). Free Word Associations Correspond to Contiguities Between Words in Texts. *Journal of Quantitative Linguistics*, 12(2-3):111–122.

Zock, M. and Bilac, S. (2004). Word Lookup on the Basis of Associations: From an Idea to a Roadmap. In *Proceedings of the Workshop on Enhancing and Using Electronic Dictionaries*.

Zock, M. and Schwab, D. (2011). Storage Does Not Guarantee Access. The Problem of Organizing and Accessing Words in a Speaker's Lexicon. *Journal of Cognitive Science*, 12(3):233–259.

Zock, M., Ferret, O., and Schwab, D. (2010). Deliberate Word Access: An Intuition, a Roadmap and Some Preliminary Empirical Results. *International Journal of Speech Technology*, 13(4):201–218.

Zock, M. (2002). Sorry, What Was Your Name Again, or How to Overcome the Tip-of-the-Tongue Problem with the Help of a Computer? In *Proceedings of the Workshop on Building and Using Semantic Networks*.

Proceedings of the 15th Workshop on Building and Using Comparable Corpora (BUCC 2022) @LREC2022 , pages 8–14
Marseille, June 25, 2022
© European Language Resources Association (ELRA), licensed under CC-BY-NC

About Evaluating Bilingual Lexicon Induction

Martin Laville[1], Emmanuel Morin[1], Philippe Langlais[2]
[1]LS2N, UMR CNRS 6004, Universite de Nantes, France
[2]RALI-DIRO, Montreal, Canada
[1]firstname.lastname@ls2n.fr, [2]felipe@iro.umontreal.ca

Abstract

With numerous new methods proposed recently, the evaluation of Bilingual Lexicon Induction have been quite hazardous and inconsistent across works. Some studies proposed some guidance to sanitize this; yet, they are not necessarily followed by practitioners. In this study, we try to gather these different recommendations and add our owns, with the aim to propose an unified evaluation protocol. We further show that the easiness of a benchmark while being correlated to the proximity of the language pairs being considered, is even more conditioned on the graphical similarities within the test word pairs.

1. Introduction

Bilingual lexicon induction (BLI) is a long studied task (Rapp, 1995; Fung, 1998) that received a lot of attention recently (Gouws and Søgaard, 2015; Artetxe et al., 2016; Ruder et al., 2019; Hakimi Parizi and Cook, 2020). Thanks to the push of deep learning and so-called word-embedding models such as word2vec (Mikolov et al., 2013a), many new approaches vivified this task.

Many methods have emerged with the goal of computing accurate representations for cross-lingual word embeddings (CLWE). Mikolov et al. (2013b) used a linear transformation to project the source language into the target one, an approach known as *mapping*. In line, Faruqui and Dyer (2014) project the source and target embeddings in a new shared vector space. Artetxe et al. (2016) proposed several constraints (orthogonality, normalization, whitening etc.) to improve the quality of mapping.

More recently, unsupervised mapping methods (Conneau et al., 2017; Artetxe et al., 2018b) have been proposed which are nowadays starting to compete with supervised one. However, as noted in Artetxe et al. (2020), unsupervised methods, although interesting from a research point of view is not a realistic setup, as it is highly unlikely to have enough data to train CLWE without the existence of a seed lexicon.

A recent trend in BLI, known as *joint-training* consists in training the source and target word embeddings at the same time. Gouws and Søgaard (2015) proposed to concatenate the source and target corpora into which they randomly selected words (source or target) that they translated, thus producing a mixed corpus used to train a single embedding space. Following this, Duong et al. (2016) used a classic CBOW (Mikolov et al., 2013a) architecture and while training select the most appropriate translation of the context word based on a seed lexicon. Also Hakimi Parizi and Cook (2020) improved this by using the fastText model (Bojanowski et al., 2016). Finally, (Wang et al., 2020) mixed joint-trained embeddings with a mapping method.

While people have been working on the BLI task for many years, and even more so recently, the evaluation of BLI has been somehow surprisingly overlooked. (Conneau et al., 2017) created (making use of an internal translation tool) the MUSE dataset: over a hundred automatically collected bilingual lexicons of up to 100k pairs of words. This dataset rapidly became the defacto benchmark for BLI.

While MUSE is an invaluable resource per see, a number of concerns about it has surfaced. For instance, Czarnowska et al. (2019) observed that MUSE mainly gathers high frequency words, while Kementchedjhieva et al. (2019) indicate that about a quarter of the content of the lexicons consists of proper nouns, often perfectly identical graphically. Arguably, translating such entities is not of the utmost practical interest and focusing on less frequent words, for which translation are likely less listed in bilingual lexicons, is of more practical value.

In this paper, we review (Section 2) the different concerns already made about the evaluation in BLI (regarding the process itself or the data used) to which we add our own observations. We describe in Section 3 the data and the BLI systems we use to illustrate the concerns from Section 2. We then present in Section 4 the results of the different experiments made and analyze them. We finally conclude in Section 5.

2. Evaluation in BLI

The MUSE dataset is a collection of multiple bilingual lexicons in different languages: German, English, Spanish, French, Italian, and Portuguese languages all paired to each others. Lexicons from 39 other languages are also paired with English, in both directions. 108 language pairs are available in total, all with train and test sets already prepared.

2.1. Part-of-Speech (PoS) and Proper Nouns

Kementchedjhieva et al. (2019) conducted a study of the composition of MUSE. They manually annotated the English to/from German, Danish, Bulgarian, Arabic and Hindi lexicons[1]. We report in Table 1 the detail

[1]https://github.com/coastalcph/MUSE_dicos

of their annotations and the comparison made with the English Web Treebank (EWT)[2], which contains gold-standard PoS tags.

	Noun	PNoun	Verb	Adj/Adv
MUSE	49.6	24.9	12.5	13.0
EWT	35.6	15.1	23.3	25.9

Table 1: English PoS percentage of 4 categories for the MUSE dataset in comparison with the EWT. After Kementchedjhieva et al. (2019).

This table indicates that the proportion of these four categories in EWT — a representative set of sentences — is not respected in MUSE; the main problem being the high proportion of proper nouns. Moreover, Kementchedjhieva et al. (2019) note that proper nouns can reference totally different entities (for example first names or surnames) making it hard to establish a real sense (Pierini, 2008) and thus, questioning the pertinence of their presence in a BLI test set. In order to correct this issue, Kementchedjhieva et al. (2019) suggest as a first step to get rid of these pairs of words to use gazetteers to filter them out.
We also point in the next section that pairs of proper nouns are made of a lot of identical words and thus propose a simple solution to correct this.

2.2. Graphical Similarities of Word Pairs

We first focus on graphically identical word pairs. We suggest that these pair of words, present in high quantity in the MUSE dataset, are for the most part not of great interest, if not incorrect (*alignbars* or *wehrmacht* as the source and target word in the French-Spanish lexicon), and propose a simple solution to solve this. We then extend on the graphically close word pairs.

2.2.1. Identical word pairs

We report in Table 2 the percentage of identical word pairs in MUSE lexicons involving the German, English, Spanish, French, Italian, and Portuguese languages. We also add some languages linked only with English such as Czech, Norwegian and Russian.
Among the different bilingual lexicons we consider, many have over 30% of identical word pairs. In particular, German-French and German-Italian with over 49%, which is clearly worrisome. However, we note that with lexicons involving English, we have the lowest percentage, suggesting either a better control has been made on the English lexicons or the greater quality/quantity of the English corpora used to generate the dataset allowed a better quality in the automatically generated lexicons. Despite this, we still find some graphically identical word pairs in the *English-Russian* lexicon whereas the two languages have a different writing system (for instance, *motors* or *teen*).

[2] https://universaldependencies.org/treebanks/en_ewt/index.html

	de	en	es	fr	it	pt	avg
de	-	18.5	29.4	49.2	49.8	46.1	38.6
en	16.0	-	16.5	21.0	21.1	18.4	18.6
es	20.3	18.4	-	30.3	31.3	47.9	29.6
fr	41.8	27.5	30.7	-	29.2	24.8	30.8
it	45.8	24.1	32.1	30.8	-	38.0	34.2
pt	40.9	21.6	47.5	27.4	41.2	-	35.7
avg	33.0	22.0	31.2	31.7	34.5	35.0	**31.3**
	en-cs		en-no		en-ru		-
	→	←	→	←	→	←	-
	16.1	17.6	26.1	36.8	2.4	0.0	-

Table 2: Percentage of pairs of graphically identical words in selected MUSE lexicons.

Taking advantage of this characteristic of MUSE is easy. For instance, Laville et al. (2020) reported that a simple approach to BLI based on this property could easily outperform mapping-based methods.
In order to understand why so many word pairs involve identical words and whether it makes sense to gather gather them in a test lexicon, we inspected the German-French and French-Spanish lexicons.
We sampled identical pairs of words and manually separated them in 4 different categories: First Names (FN), Named Entities (NE) (brand, geographical entities or names such as "Roosevelt"), Doubtful (D) (*e.g.*, *#ffffff* or words from other languages, mostly English: *spirit* or *biography*). The remaining pairs being categorized as correct (C). The results of this annotation are presented in Table 3.

	FN	NE	D (EN pairs)	C	Total
de-fr	17.1	28.8	48.9 (21.0)	5.2	767
fr-es	19.6	33.5	40.9 (20.9)	6.0	465

Table 3: Sample of graphically identical word pairs in the German-French and French-Spanish lexicons and their manual classification.

The FN and NE categories can be seen as sub-parts of the PNoun PoS tag, however, we decided to separate them because of what they really represent. As exposed earlier, FN (such as *Federico* or *Bryan*) do not represent much interest in a BLI task because they do not convey any real sense. However, for the NE part, if obtaining the equivalent in an other language (we can not say translation here) for a named entity can be of interest in some scenario, it seems more suited to a bilingual version of a Named-Entity Recognition task than to BLI. We add that a major part of this category is made of cities or regions from Germany (*Gelsenkirchen*), France (*Orléans*) or other countries (*Lugano*, *Nebraska*). The pairs of words we classified as Doubtful are mostly made of words from other languages (for instance *freedom*, or *musica*) but also acronyms such as *nva* (a Belgium political party), and thus are arguably of no compelling interest for evaluating BLI. Finally, we note some pair of words made of real perfect cognates (for instance *terminal* is present in

both the German-French and French-Spanish lexicons) but they only represent 5% of identical word pairs we sampled.
Thanks to the available proper nouns lists created by (Kementchedjhieva et al., 2019) on three language pairs with identical writing system (*English* to and from *Danish, German and Spanish*), we measure that 86% of the proper noun pairs are made of identical words (*Tennessee* or *Georges*).
Thus, we argue that a major part of graphically identical words are mainly of no interest in a BLI evaluating setting. Since we measured that only 5% of identical word pairs present a real interest, we suggest to getting rid of them while evaluating BLI, which will incidentally correct the problem of the proportion of proper nouns we discussed in Section 2.1.

2.2.2. Graphically close word pairs

We now take a look at graphically close pairs. After the removal of the identical word pairs, there is still an average of 40.1% word pairs with a Levenshtein distance of at most 3[3]. If we can logically note the proportion being higher between romance language (*Portuguese-Spanish*; 69.8% or *Italian-French*: 57.2%), it is surprising to see pairs such as *Italian-English* (46.5%) or *French-English* (44.4%) sharing that much similarities in their vocabulary, despite French and Italian being Romance languages while English is a Germanic one.
As the lexicons are made of a lot of graphically close words, we suggest, in addition to the evaluation on the lexicons without identical pairs, to split the lexicons in two sublists using the Levenshtein distance. We show later in Section 4 that the graphic proximity of the pair of words is a major factor in the success of the systems.

2.3. The *Morph* Dataset

Czarnowska et al. (2019) points three main problems with the existing datasets and MUSE: the lack of diversity in the frequency of the words, the fact that a word and its inflections can appear in both the train and test set (semantic leakage), and finally the lack of morphological diversity in most of the existing datasets. With the objectives of solving those problems, Czarnowska et al. (2019) introduce a new dataset to evaluate BLI, containing morphologically complete lexicons for 5 Slavic (Polish, Czech, Russian, Slovak, and Ukrainian) and 5 Romance (French, Spanish, Italian, Portuguese, and Catalan) languages. The lexicons are in every directions for both Slavic and Romance separately (meaning there is no dictionary from a Romance language to a Slavic and vice versa). We refer to them as *Morph* in the following.
Frequency Range: historically, BLI has mostly been focused on high frequency words. For instance, Mikolov et al. (2013b) used the $6k$ most frequent words to construct their training and test lexicons. Similarly, Czarnowska et al. (2019) reports that the pairs of words in the test lexicon of the MUSE dataset are all coming from the $10k$ most frequent source words. As Jakubina and Langlais (2017) empirically showed, it is far more difficult to identify translations of less frequent words, while we argue is a more sensible task (translations of common words are likely already listed in existing dictionaries). The *Morph* dataset is far more diverse on the frequency of its word pairs, containing, for the French-Spanish pair, 1 163 pairs of words with a source word from the top $10k$ of the vocabulary, but also (for instance) 1 126 pairs in the $500 - 600k$ range.
Semantic Leakage: Czarnowska et al. (2019) indicate that MUSE suffers of semantic leakage, meaning it is common for a word to appear in the training part of the lexicon as well as in the test part with a different inflection. In the *Morph* dataset the separation is done cleanly between the training and the testing part of the lexicons, because it is done on the lemmata, preventing the possibility of having two different inflections of a same word in the two lexicons.
Morphological Diversity: finally, the authors indicate that most words in MUSE has only one inflection form, while their dictionary is looking to have the best possible coverage for each lemmata. For instance, in the French-Spanish lexicon, the French verb *injecter* have 46 different inflections (from the first-person present tense *injecte* to the very seldom simple past form *injectâtes*).
The *Morph* lexicons present many interesting characteristics, however we point some problems. First, they do not come usable as is: if the presence of multiple inflections for each lemmata is an interesting feature, we think that being able to find them all, and particularly when there is that many (often out of use), is not the first objective of BLI. Thus, we recommend the usage of lemmata only.
In a similar vein, the high quantity of proposed translation lemmata per source lemmata is not really suited to a BLI task. For instance, the verb *abandonner* in French has 21 different candidates lemmata in Italian (*abortire, allentare, arrendere, bandire, cedere, concedere, defezionare, demordere, desistere, disertare, fermare, interrompere, liberare, mollare, piantare, recedere, rinunciare, rinunziare, sfollare, sgomberare, sgombrare*), and we think that finding 21 different translations for a single word is not what BLI is about.
About semantic leakage, we also point that, as the author indicate, a human translator is able to find more complex forms such as a first-person plural future form *hablarámos* thanks to their knowledge of the canonical form *hablar*. Thus, we argue that semantic leakage should not be seen as problematic in BLI as it is very similar to this case.
While *Morph* presents less languages pairs than MUSE, we strongly recommend its use whenever possible, as we do next. Last, we note that in their work, Czarnowska et al. (2019) only evaluate *Morph* using

[3]A threshold we found empirically as the best way to separate pairs of cognates.

P@1, while we show in the next section that MAP would be much more relevant.

2.4. Mean Average Precision (MAP) vs Precision at rank k (P@k)

While most works in BLI use P@k (typically with $k \in \{1, 5, 10\}$) to evaluate the quality of their method, Glavaš et al. (2019) advocate for the use of MAP instead. They point that MAP is more informative, because in P@k, a model that ranks a correct translation at $k + 1$ is equally penalised as the model that ranks it at rank $k + 1000$, while MAP gives a reward based on the rank.

In addition to that, they point that using MAP with only one correct translation per query is equivalent to the Mean Reciprocal Rank. However, we stress that MUSE proposes multiple valid translations per source word and therefore, their remark does not apply here. To show this, we report the ratio of target word per source word in Table 4. We indicate this for the lexicons from and to English, but also for the lexicons that do not include English in addition to the average per lexicon.

	en-x	x-en	incl. en	no en	avg
ratio	1.73	1.61	1.67	1.09	1.58

Table 4: Ratio of target words per source word in the MUSE dataset.

When using P@k, the evaluation system is just looking for the best ranked correct translation, leaving aside all the other ones. For instance, for a source word with 2 proposed translations, a system ranking one translation at top 1 and the other at top 2 $\{1, 2\}$ will be rewarded the same as a system ranking $\{1, 1000\}$ in P@1, while it will only be fully rewarded on the first case using MAP. Thereby, while using P@k, the presence of multiple translations in the lexicons does not become the assurance of a system of quality that takes into account polysemy as it will only look for one translation, which is obviously easier than finding them all.

We elaborate more on this problem by indicating that the ignored words in the case of multiple correct translations amplifies the problem of low frequency words or graphically distant pairs, as most systems are likely to find the higher frequency or the graphically closer translations first[4].

Thus, we strongly agree with Glavaš et al. (2019), and highly recommend the usage of MAP over P@k when evaluating BLI.

3. Protocol

In this section we briefly present the data and the two BLI methods we use to support the points discussed in Section 2.

[4]We back this claim with experiments in Section 4

3.1. Data

We use five different Wikipedia corpora as our training data: English, French, Italian, Russian and Spanish. We extracted the corpora using the WikiExtractor tool (Attardi, 2015).

We used the MUSE training part of the dataset when a training lexicon was needed.

3.2. BLI Methods

We compare two representative BLI methods that we now describe.

Mapping method Mapping (or alignment) methods consist in two steps. First, an embedding space is learnt separately for the source and target languages. We use fastText to train embeddings on the Wikipedia corpora. Second, a projection matrix is learned to map one language embedding space into the second one, allowing the comparison between languages. We use the VecMap tool (Artetxe et al., 2018a) as our mapping method.

Joint-training method Joint-training methods consist in the following steps. First, a bilingual corpus is build by concatenating both the source and target ones in order to create a shared vocabulary across languages. Then, the training of the embeddings for the two languages at the same time on the concatenated bilingual corpus, followed by the separation of embeddings into their original vocabulary. We use the *joint_align* framework (Wang et al., 2020) to do so. It also uses fastText to train the embeddings.

Wang et al. (2020) improved joint-training by adding a vocabulary reallocation phase such that, if an anchor word (i.e. a word graphically identical that appear in both part of the corpus and thus is only represented by one vector in the shared vocabulary) appears mostly in a language it is removed from the shared vocabulary in order to obtain a more precise representation during the mapping phase. For the alignment method, they use RCSLS (Joulin et al., 2018), which we follow.

3.3. Ranking of Candidates

Once the embeddings have been trained and projected in a shared space and in order to rank the candidates, we measure the similarity between every source word of the test dictionary with every target vocabulary word. We use the $CSLS$ (Conneau et al., 2017), an adaptation of the cosine similarity which reduces hubness[5], to order them:

$$CSLS(w_s, w_t) = 2\cos(w_s, w_t) - \text{knn}(w_s) - \text{knn}(w_t) \quad (1)$$

where w_s and w_t are the source and target word vectors, and $\text{knn}(x)$ is a function that measures the mean cosine similarity between x and its k nearest neighbors.

[5]Words that tend to be the translation of many others.

		MUSE						*Morph*			
		es-fr	fr-it	it-es	en-ru	en-fr	avg	es-fr	fr-it	it-es	avg
Mapping	P@1	84.6	80.5	87.1	44.9	78.8	75.2	57.6	61.9	55.9	58.5
	MAP	87.9	84.4	87.3	51.3	72.8	76.7	45.0	48.7	45.8	46.5
Joint-Training	P@1	65.9	62.6	70.6	34.7	64.5	60.0	43.5	55.3	46.2	48.3
	MAP	71.8	67.5	73.7	39.8	61.1	62.8	37.3	44.8	41.4	41.2
Ratio target / source words		1.02	1.02	1.16	1.63	1.96	1.36	3.37	3.68	2.63	3.22

Table 5: Detailed results of the mapping and joint-training methods with MAP and P@1 metrics.

4. Experiments

From the *Morph* dataset, we considered the *Italian-Spanish*, *Spanish-French*, and *French-Italian* lexicons which have respectively 1 761, 1 173 and 2 273 source words. We selected the same language pairs from the MUSE dataset, as well as the *English-Russian* lexicon where the two languages have a different writing system, and finally the *English-French* pair. Each MUSE lexicon gathers around 1 500 source words.

4.1. P@1 vs MAP

We report in Table 5 the results obtained when using P@1 or MAP, the last row of the table indicates the ratio of target words per source word.

In Section 2.4, we reported that Glavaš et al. (2019) advocate for MAP because it is more informative, essentially because it takes into account all the proposed valid translations, and not just the highest ranked. This table confirms this claim and shows that the results in P@1 are higher than MAP when there is multiple possible translations, while MAP becomes higher whenever the target-to-source ratio tends to 1.

One notable exception however is for *English-Russian*, where the MAP is above P@1 despite a ratio of 1.63. This can be explained by a P@5 of 72.0 (+27 points from P@1), meaning that the system find a good part of the correct translations between the second and fifth rank, which is rewarded by the MAP. While for other languages, the P@5 is usually better than P@1 by at most 10 points.

And thus, it shows that having multiple possible translations artificially improves the P@k whereas intuitively, the introduction of polysemy should make it harder to find all the translations. Following this, we report only MAP results next.

4.2. Graphically Close Words

In Table 7, we report the results on different lexicons. In the first sublists (*not id.*), we remove all the graphically identical word pairs, as we suggested in Section 2.2. Then, we split these sublists based on Levenshtein distance: *Far* contains pairs of words with a distance over 3, while the sublist *Close* gathers close word pairs (distance less than 4).

This table clearly indicates that for both methods, it is much easier to conduct BLI on graphically close word pairs. If we let aside the *English-Russian* lexicon[6], the difference between the *Far* and *Close* sublists goes from 8 points (*es-fr* with joint-training on MUSE) up to 50 points (*it-es* with mapping on *Morph*).

Since popular reference lexicons such as MUSE are built largely from similar word pairs, performances reported on this dataset are in a way optimistic, and reporting results on both *Far* and *Close* lists as we did here is we believe a good practice.

4.3. Analysis

We show in Table 6 some output of the VecMap system for three hand-picked source words, along their rank in the list of proposed candidates, as well as their number of occurrences in the target corpus. This table supports the idea that in the case of multiple possible translations, the first target word found will likely be the graphically close or very frequent; and thus with P@1, the system will not be evaluated much on its ability to handle rare or graphically distant words.

On the *English-French* lexicon, 802 source words have at least 2 candidate translations. For 69% of the source word, the best ranked candidates was the most frequent one, for 74% it was the graphically closest with the source word and it was the most frequent and graphically closest one for 51% of the source words.

Source word	Target word	Rank	#occ.
customs	coutumes	1	7221
	douanes	2	4165
arch	arche	1	7407
	voûte	3	541
reveal	révéler	1	7577
	dévoiler	5	1858

Table 6: Some candidates proposed by the mapping method.

Figure 1 shows the correlation between the MAP and the average Levenshtein distance between word pairs of the test lexicon. It shows that the difficulty of the task does not only correlate with the diversity of the pair of languages considered, but also from the graphical proximity of word pairs. *English-Russian* are two languages that present many more differences than

[6]Those languages have different writing systems and thus variations in the Levenshtein distance mainly come from the length of the words.

		MUSE						*Morph*			
		es-fr	fr-it	it-es	en-ru	en-fr	avg	es-fr	fr-it	it-es	avg
Mapping	*not id.*	88.5	84.0	84.2	50.9	63.8	74.3	41.4	47.5	36.0	41.6
	Far	78.9	71.3	63.3	51.4	46.8	62.3	16.2	19.7	11.5	15.8
	Close	91.2	88.7	87.6	36.4	68.3	74.4	62.9	71.4	58.9	64.4
Joint-Training	*not id.*	68.6	64.0	67.1	39.3	48.9	57.6	33.3	43.4	30.5	35.7
	Far	62.4	55.1	52.8	40.1	35.4	49.2	13.9	19.7	10.6	14.7
	Close	70.4	67.3	69.4	33.7	53.1	58.8	49.0	63.5	45.9	52.8

Table 7: MAP results when test lexicons are split based on the graphical proximity of their word pairs.

French-Italian, but as the *Morph* lexicons are made of very few graphically close word pairs (and thus have a high average of Levenshtein distance), the systems does not perform well in both case.

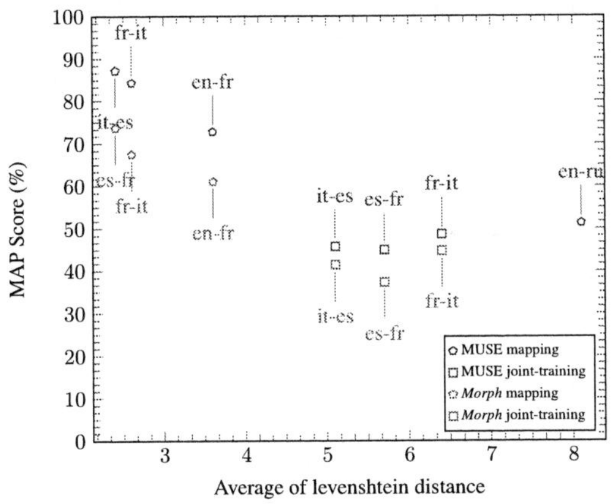

Figure 1: MAP versus Levenshtein distance of test word pairs.

5. Conclusion

In this work, we discuss different studies on BLI evaluation and add our own findings. We articulate a number of concerns that should guide BLI evaluation, leading us to formulate recommendations that are intended — we believe — to target what matters in practice; notably the ability to handle graphically distant pair of words.
First, using MUSE as an evaluation dataset, we recommend the removal of graphically identical pair of words. As we have seen in Section 2, they represent a major part of the MUSE lexicons and are often not interesting or even incorrect word pairs. Second, and if the language pairs allow it, we recommend an evaluation on both MUSE and *Morph*. Then, and for both dataset, we recommend that the lexicons should be evaluated as a whole but also in two groups based on the Levenshtein distance. The results presented in Section 4 show that for both type of methods (mapping or joint-training), the systems perform way better on close pair of words.
Also, we endorse the usage of MAP over P@k, especially if multiple candidate translations per source words are available, as it will be way more representative of the capacity a system to handle polysemy.
Finally, we highly recommend a more thorough evaluation than just looking at the MAP alone, and selecting a few pair of words with different characteristics can give great insights on the reality of the quality of the system and what are its strengths and weaknesses.

Bibliographical References

Artetxe, M., Labaka, G., and Agirre, E. (2016). Learning principled bilingual mappings of word embeddings while preserving monolingual invariance. In *Proceedings of the 2016 Conference on Empirical Methods in Natural Language Processing (EMNLP)*, pages 2289–2294, Austin, TX, USA.

Artetxe, M., Labaka, G., and Agirre, E. (2018a). Generalizing and improving bilingual word embedding mappings with a multi-step framework of linear transformations. In *Proceedings of the Thirty-Second AAAI Conference on Artificial Intelligence (AAAI'18)*, pages 5012–5019, New Orleans, LA, USA.

Artetxe, M., Labaka, G., and Agirre, E. (2018b). A robust self-learning method for fully unsupervised cross-lingual mappings of word embeddings. In *Proceedings of the 56th Annual Meeting of the Association for Computational Linguistics (ACL'18)*, pages 789–798, Melbourne, Australia.

Artetxe, M., Ruder, S., Yogatama, D., Labaka, G., and Agirre, E. (2020). A call for more rigor in unsupervised cross-lingual learning. *Proceedings of the 58th Annual Meeting of the Association for Computational Linguistics.*

Attardi, G. (2015). Wikiextractor. `https://github.com/attardi/wikiextractor`.

Bojanowski, P., Grave, E., Joulin, A., and Mikolov, T. (2016). Enriching word vectors with subword information. *CoRR*, abs/1607.04606.

Conneau, A., Lample, G., Ranzato, M., Denoyer, L., and Jégou, H. (2017). Word translation without parallel data. *CoRR*, abs/1710.04087.

Czarnowska, P., Ruder, S., Grave, E., Cotterell, R., and Copestake, A. (2019). Don't forget the long tail! a comprehensive analysis of morphological generalization in bilingual lexicon induction. In *Proceedings of the 2019 Conference on Empirical Methods in Natural Language Processing and the 9th International Joint Conference on Natural Language Processing (EMNLP-IJCNLP)*, pages 974–983, Hong Kong, China, November. Association for Computational Linguistics.

Duong, L., Kanayama, H., Ma, T., Bird, S., and Cohn, T. (2016). Learning crosslingual word embeddings without bilingual corpora. In *Proceedings of the 2016 Conference on Empirical Methods in Natural Language Processing (EMNLP'16)*, pages 1285–1295, Austin, TX, USA, November.

Faruqui, M. and Dyer, C. (2014). Improving Vector Space Word Representations Using Multilingual Correlation. In *Proceedings of the 14th Conference of the European Chapter of the Association for Computational Linguistics (EACL'14)*, pages 462–471, Gothenburg, Sweden.

Fung, P. (1998). A Statistical View on Bilingual Lexicon Extraction: From Parallel Corpora to Nonparallel Corpora. In *Proceedings of the 3rd Conference of the Association for Machine Translation in the Americas on Machine Translation and the Information Soup (AMTA'98)*, pages 1–17, Langhorne, PA, USA.

Glavaš, G., Litschko, R., Ruder, S., and Vulić, I. (2019). How to (properly) evaluate cross-lingual word embeddings: On strong baselines, comparative analyses, and some misconceptions. In *Proceedings of the 57th Annual Meeting of the Association for Computational Linguistics*, pages 710–721, Florence, Italy, July. Association for Computational Linguistics.

Gouws, S. and Søgaard, A. (2015). Simple task-specific bilingual word embeddings. In *Proceedings of the 2015 Conference of the North American Chapter of the Association for Computational Linguistics: Human Language Technologies (NAACL-HLT'15)*, pages 1386–1390, Denver, CO, USA, May–June.

Hakimi Parizi, A. and Cook, P. (2020). Joint training for learning cross-lingual embeddings with sub-word information without parallel corpora. In *Proceedings of the Ninth Joint Conference on Lexical and Computational Semantics (*SEM'20)*, pages 39–49, Barcelona, Spain (Online), December.

Jakubina, L. and Langlais, P. (2017). Reranking translation candidates produced by several bilingual word similarity sources. In *Proceedings of the 15th Conference of the European Chapter of the Association for Computational Linguistics: Volume 2, Short Papers*, pages 605–611, Valencia, Spain, April. Association for Computational Linguistics.

Joulin, A., Bojanowski, P., Mikolov, T., Jégou, H., and Grave, E. (2018). Loss in translation: Learning bilingual word mapping with a retrieval criterion. In *Proceedings of the 2018 Conference on Empirical Methods in Natural Language Processing*, pages 2979–2984, Brussels, Belgium, October-November. Association for Computational Linguistics.

Kementchedjhieva, Y., Hartmann, M., and Søgaard, A. (2019). Lost in evaluation: Misleading benchmarks for bilingual dictionary induction. In *Proceedings of the 2019 Conference on Empirical Methods in Natural Language Processing and the 9th International Joint Conference on Natural Language Processing (EMNLP-IJCNLP)*, pages 3336–3341, Hong Kong, China, November. Association for Computational Linguistics.

Laville, M., Hazem, A., and Morin, E. (2020). TALN/LS2N participation at the BUCC shared task: Bilingual dictionary induction from comparable corpora. In *Proceedings of the 13th Workshop on Building and Using Comparable Corpora (BUCC'20)*, pages 56–60, Marseille, France, May.

Mikolov, T., Chen, K., Corrado, G., and Dean, J. (2013a). Efficient estimation of word representations in vector space.

Mikolov, T., Le, Q. V., and Sutskever, I. (2013b). Exploiting similarities among languages for machine translation. *CoRR*, abs/1309.4168.

Pierini, P. (2008). Opening a pandora's box: Proper names in english phraseology. *Linguistik Online*, 36, 10.

Rapp, R. (1995). Identify Word Translations in Non-Parallel Texts. In *Proceedings of the 35th Annual Meeting of the Association for Computational Linguistics (ACL'95)*, pages 320–322, Boston, MA, USA.

Ruder, S., Vulić, I., and Søgaard, A. (2019). A survey of cross-lingual word embedding models. *Journal of Artificial Intelligence Research*, 65:569–631.

Wang, Z., Xie, J., Xu, R., Yang, Y., Neubig, G., and Carbonell, J. (2020). Cross-lingual alignment vs joint training: A comparative study and a simple unified framework.

Proceedings of the 15th Workshop on Building and Using Comparable Corpora (BUCC 2022) @LREC2022, pages 15–22
Marseille, June 25, 2022
© European Language Resources Association (ELRA), licensed under CC-BY-NC

Don't Forget Cheap Training Signals Before Building Unsupervised Bilingual Word Embeddings

Silvia Severini, Viktor Hangya, Masoud Jalili Sabet, Alexander Fraser, Hinrich Schütze
Center for Information and Language Processing
LMU Munich, Germany
{silvia, hangyav, masoud, fraser}@cis.uni-muenchen.de

Abstract

Bilingual Word Embeddings (BWEs) are one of the cornerstones of cross-lingual transfer of NLP models. They can be built using only monolingual corpora without supervision leading to numerous works focusing on unsupervised BWEs. However, most of the current approaches to build unsupervised BWEs do not compare their results with methods based on easy-to-access cross-lingual signals. In this paper, we argue that such signals should always be considered when developing unsupervised BWE methods. The two approaches we find most effective are: 1) using identical words as seed lexicons (which unsupervised approaches incorrectly assume are not available for orthographically distinct language pairs) and 2) combining such lexicons with pairs extracted by matching romanized versions of words with an edit distance threshold. We experiment on thirteen non-Latin languages (and English) and show that such cheap signals work well and that they outperform using more complex unsupervised methods on distant language pairs such as Chinese, Japanese, Kannada, Tamil, and Thai. In addition, they are even competitive with the use of high-quality lexicons in supervised approaches. Our results show that these training signals should not be neglected when building BWEs, even for distant languages.

Keywords: Bilingual Word Embeddings, Bilingual Dictionary Induction, Romanization

1. Introduction

Bilingual Word Embeddings (BWEs) are useful for many cross-lingual tasks. They can be built effectively even when only a small seed lexicon is available by mapping monolingual embeddings into a shared space. This makes them particularly valuable for low-resource settings (Mikolov et al., 2013). In addition, unsupervised mapping approaches can build BWEs for some languages when no seed lexicon is available. Various unsupervised methods have been proposed relying on the assumption that embedding spaces are isomorphic (Zhang et al., 2017; Lample et al., 2018; Artetxe et al., 2018; Alvarez-Melis and Jaakkola, 2018; Chen and Cardie, 2018; Hoshen and Wolf, 2018; Mohiuddin and Joty, 2019; Alaux et al., 2019; Dou et al., 2020; Grave et al., 2019; Li et al., 2020). However, with one exception, none of them compare their results with the widely available baseline of using identical words as seed lexicons.

It has been shown that identical word pairs of two languages can be used to build high quality BWEs (Smith et al., 2017; Artetxe et al., 2017). However, they were only tested on language pairs with similar scripts. The only exception is the work of Søgaard et al. (2018), who tested identical word pairs on English and Greek which use different alphabetical characters but the same numerals. Regardless of these experiments, recent works still propose novel unsupervised approaches without considering such cheap training signals, at least as baseline systems (Mohiuddin and Joty, 2019; Alaux et al., 2019; Dou et al., 2020; Grave et al., 2019; Li et al., 2020).

In this paper however, we argue that such signals should be used as a cheap and effective baseline in the development of future unsupervised methods. We define them cheap as they require widely available monolingual corpora only, e.g., Wikipedia dumps, but no parallel data. We study two approaches for extracting the initial seed lexicons to build BWEs without relying on expensive dictionaries. (1) First, we leverage identical pairs as proposed by Smith et al. (2017; Artetxe et al. (2017). Previous work assumed such pairs not to be available for language pairs with distinct scripts, hence the development of various unsupervised mapping approaches. We show that, surprisingly, they do appear in large quantities in the monolingual corpora that we use, even for distinct-script pairs. In contrast to Søgaard et al. (2018), we test identical word pairs on multiple language pairs with distinct scripts, including pairs using distinct numerals. In addition, we propose to (2) strengthen identical pairs by extending them with further easily accessible pairs based on romanization and edit distance, which exploits implicit links between languages in the form of approximate word transliteration pairs.

We focus on distant language pairs having distinct scripts for many of which unsupervised approaches have failed or had very poor performance so far. For instance, English to Chinese, Japanese, Kannada, Tamil, and Thai, which all obtain a score close to 0 on the Bilingual Dictionary Induction (BDI) task (Vulić et al., 2019). We evaluate the two approaches on thirteen different non-Latin[1] languages paired with English on BDI. We compare our lexicons' performance with unsupervised mapping and the frequently used MUSE training lexi-

[1]We use *(non-)Latin language* here as a short form for *language standardly written in a (non-)Latin script.*

cons (Lample et al., 2018) and show that our noisy word pairs make it possible to build BWEs for language pairs where unsupervised approaches failed before and give accuracy scores similar to high quality lexicons.
Our work calls into question – at least for BDI – the strong trend toward unsupervised approaches in recent literature, similarly to Vulić et al. (2019), given that cheap signals are (i) available and easy to exploit, (ii) sufficient to obtain performance similar to dictionaries based on parallel resources like MUSE and (iii) able to make up for the failure of unsupervised methods. Finally, we analyze which lexicon properties impact performance and show that our lexicon outperform unsupervised methods also for non-English language pairs. Our paper calls for the need to use easily accessible bilingual signals, such as identical and/or transliteration word pairs, as baselines when developing unsupervised BWE approaches.

2. Unsupervised pair extraction

We show that we can extract the seed lexicon needed for mapping systems without the need for labeled data, making up for the failure of unsupervised methods. First, we show that identical pairs do appear in corpora of distant languages and can be exploited. Secondly, we propose a novel method to boost the identical pairs sets by extracting the initial seed lexicon without the need for any bilingual knowledge, starting from monolingual corpora, and using romanization and edit distance.

2.1. Identical pair approach

When dealing with languages with different scripts, identical pairs would seem to be unlikely to occur, which is assumed by unsupervised mapping methods. Smith et al. (2017; Artetxe et al. (2017) form dictionaries from identical strings which appear in both languages but limit their approach to similar languages sharing a common alphabet, such as European ones. Similarly, (Lample et al., 2018) refrain from using such identical word pairs, assuming they are not available for distant languages. An exception is the work of Søgaard et al. (2018) which shows the presence of identical pairs between English and Greek, which share numerals only but not alphabetical characters.
However, we show that there are domains where these pairs are actually available in large quantity even for pairs with different scripts, including the use of different numerals; an example is Wikipedia: see the statistics of fastText Wikipedia embeddings (Bojanowski et al., 2017) in Table 1. Most of these identical pairs are punctuation marks and digits, non-transliterated named entities written in the Latin script, or English words (assumingly words of a title) which were not translated in the non-English languages. This is also true for language pairs not including English. In this paper, we build BWEs based on these pairs and show that they are sufficient for good BDI results on distant language pairs with distinct scripts.

Lang	ID	Lang	ID	Lang	ID
ko-th*	17K	ko-he*	11K	he-th*	15K
en-zh*	62K	en-bn*	31K	en-ar*	19K
en-th	46K	en-hi*	30K	en-ru	18K
en-ja	43K	en-ta*	23K	en-he*	17K
en-el	35K	en-kn*	21K	en-ko*	15K
en-fa*	32K				

Table 1: Number of identical pairs per language pair. Language pairs using different digits as their official numerals, on top of different alphabetical characters, are indicated with *.

2.2. Romanization based augmentation (ID++)

Identical pairs are noisy and may appear in smaller quantities for certain corpora and language pairs (e.g., he-ko). We propose our romanization approach that builds the seed lexicon completely automatically and can augment the identical pairs set. We exploit the concept of transliteration and orthographic similarity to find a cheap signal between languages (cf. (Riley and Gildea, 2018; Severini et al., 2020a; Severini et al., 2020b; Severini et al., 2022)) and to take advantage of cognates (Chakravarthi et al., 2019; Laville et al., 2020). It consists of 3 steps at the end of which we add the identical pairs and run VecMap in a semi-supervised setting.

1. Source candidates First, we generate a list of source language words, which are the candidates to be matched with a word on the target side. We use the English Wikipedia dumps[2] as our monolingual corpus and apply Flair (Akbik et al., 2018) to extract Universal Part-of-Speech (UPOS) tags. We collect all English proper nouns (PROPN), since names are often transliterated between languages. The resulting English proper noun set consists of ≈800K words.

2. Target candidates The language-specific target data is extracted from the vocabulary of the pre-trained Wikipedia fastText embeddings (Bojanowski et al., 2017). The sets are not pre-processed with a POS tagger assuming that such a tool is missing or perform poorly for low-resource languages. Compared to the English proper noun set, the vocabularies are smaller: between 40K and 500K. Then, we romanize the corpora to obtain equivalent words but with only Latin characters – this supports the distance-based metrics in step (3). We use Uroman (Hermjakob et al., 2018) for romanization. Examples of romanization are карл (Russian)→ carl and βαβυλών (Greek) → babylon. Uroman mainly covers 1-1 character correspondences and does not vocalize words for Arabic and Hebrew. In general, its romanization is not as accurate as the transliteration of a neural model. However, neural models need a training corpus of labeled pairs to work well, while Uroman only

[2]https://dumps.wikimedia.org/ (01.04.2020)

	en-th	en-ja	en-kn	en-ta	en-zh
Unsupervised					
1.	0.00	0.96	0.00	0.07	0.07
2.	0.00	0.48	0.00	0.07	0.00
3.	0.00	0.00	0.00	0.00$^\diamond$	0.00
Semi-supervised (Artetxe et al., 2018)					
ID	24.40	48.87	22.03	17.93	37.00
Rom.	23.33	48.46	22.90	18.00	0.27
ID++	23.47	49.14	24.23	18.20	35.00
MUSE	24.33	48.73	23.78	18.80	36.53

Table 2: acc@1 on BDI for unsupervised (1: Artetxe et al. (2018), 2: Grave et al. (2019), 3: Mohiuddin and Joty (2019)) and semi-supervised approaches for 5 languages for which unsupervised methods fail. The semi-supervised results are obtained using VecMap with three different initial lexicons: the identical pair set (ID), ID extended with romanization based pairs (ID++) and the MUSE dictionary. We show an ablation study as well, i.e., the romanized pairs only (Rom.). Scores from Mohiuddin et al. (2020) are marked with $^\diamond$.

uses the character descriptions from the Unicode table,[3] manually created tables and some heuristics, supporting a large number of languages.

3. Candidate matching To find the corresponding target word for an English noun, the noun is compared with each (romanized) target word based on their orthography. The similarity of two words w_1 and w_2 is defined as $1 - \text{NL}(w_1, w_2)$, where NL is the Levenshtein distance (Levenshtein, 1966) divided by the length of the longer string. We select a pair of words if the similarity is ≥ 0.8; this ensures a trade off between number of pairs and quality, based on manual investigation. We use the Symmetric Delete algorithm to speed up computation, similarly to (Riley and Gildea, 2018). It takes the lists of source and target words, and a constant k and identifies all the source-target pairs that are identical after k insertion or deletions.[4] The final step is to look up, for each romanized target word, its original non-romanized form.

3. Evaluation

We evaluate our seed lexicons on BDI to show the quality of the BWEs obtained with them. Recent papers (Marchisio et al., 2020) show that there is a direct relationship between BDI accuracy and downstream BLEU for machine translation. Moreover, Sabet et al. (2020) show that good-quality word embeddings directly reflect the performance also for extrinsic tasks like word alignment. We use the VecMap tool to build BWEs since it supports both unsupervised, semi-supervised and supervised techniques (Artetxe et al., 2018). The semi-supervised approach is of particular interest to us since it performs well with small and noisy seed lexicons by iteratively refining them. VecMap iterates over two steps: embedding mapping and dictionary induction. The process starts from an initial dictionary that is iteratively augmented and refined by extracting probable word pairs from the BWEs built in the current iteration with BDI. The method is repeated until the improvement on the average dot product for the induced dictionary stays above a given threshold. We use pre-trained Wikipedia fastText embeddings (Bojanowski et al., 2017) as the input monolingual vectors, taking only the 200K most frequent words and using default parameters otherwise. We compare the performance of VecMap using our lexicons with MUSE. MUSE contains dictionaries for many languages and it was created using a Facebook internal translation tool (Lample et al., 2018), thus it can be considered as a higher quality cross-lingual resource based on parallel data. Since Kannada is not supported by MUSE, we use the dictionary provided by Anzer et al. (2020). We show $acc@1$ scores based on CSLS vector similarity calculated by the MUSE evaluation tool (Lample et al., 2018).[5]

Tables 2 and 3 show accuracy for all language pairs considering English as the source; see Table 7 in Appendix B for the full table containing results in both directions. Table 2 gives scores for language pairs for which unsupervised methods completely diverge (acc@1 < 1). We report results for three unsupervised methods (Artetxe et al., 2018; Mohiuddin and Joty, 2019; Grave et al., 2019). In contrast, using identical word pairs as lexicon (ID) or its extension with the romanizetion based pairs (ID++) with VecMap leads to successful BWEs without any parallel data or manually created lexicons. In addition, scores are even comparable to high-quality dictionaries like MUSE. Looking at results for all language pairs in Table 2 and 3, our sets always obtain results comparable to MUSE (baseline dictionaries), with improvements for Arabic, Chinese, Russian and Greek. In the unsupervised cases (Table 2), both ID and ID++ pair sets lead to an accuracy improvement of at least 17 points. ID++ outperform ID for three of the five low-resource pairs and five out of eight high-resource pairs proving that the romanized pairs can indeed strengthen the identical pairs sets. These results show that good quality BWEs can be built by relying on implicit cross-lingual signals without expensive supervision or fragile unsupervised approaches.

MUSE test w/o proper nouns The work of Kementchedjhieva et al. (2019) highlights that MUSE test sets contain a high number of proper nouns for German, Danish, Bulgarian, Arabic and Hindi. Since our romanization augmentation is based on such names, we evaluate their performance on the subsets of MUSE test

[3] http://unicode.org/Public/UNIDATA/UnicodeData.txt

[4] We used minimum frequency and minimum length equal to 1, k equals to 2.

[5] We follow Artetxe et al. (2018) work for comparison reasons and did not remove identical pairs from the test sets. However, overlaps between train romanized lexicons and test lexicons correspond to less than 1%.

	Unsup.	ID	Rom.	ID++	MUSE
en-ar	36.30	40.27	39.33	40.20	39.87
en-hi	40.20	40.47	39.60	40.20	40.33
en-ru	44.80	49.13	48.87	49.53	48.80
en-el	47.90	47.87	48.00	48.27	48.00
en-fa	36.70	37.67	36.80	37.67	38.00
en-he	44.60	44.47	44.53	44.67	45.00
en-bn	18.20	19.87	19.80	20.13	21.60
en-ko	19.80	27.92	28.40	28.81	28.94

Table 3: acc@1 on BDI for (best) unsupervised method and semi-supervised VecMap with different initial lexicons. (full table in Appendix B, Table 7).

	Unsup.	ID	Rom.	ID++	PanLex
th-ko	0.00	2.81	3.37	3.09	2.95
th-he	0.00	9.75	0.00	8.86	10.13
ko-th	0.00	15.90	14.23	15.26	14.36
ko-he	14.62	15.68	16.08	16.00	15.11
he-th	0.00	16.42	0.00	16.54	17.90
he-ko	14.30	15.39	15.15	15.09	16.06

Table 4: acc@1 on BDI for unsupervised and semi-supervised VecMap for all combinations of Korean, Hebrew, and Thai. PanLex are results obtained with training lexicons from Vulić et al. (2019) and semi-supervised VecMap.

sets that don't contain proper nouns. We remove proper nouns using the list of names obtained in Section 2.2 and evaluate the performance of all the approaches presented above. The new sets contains 10% less pairs on average. Results are shown in Table 8, Appendix C. The performance is similar to the one obtained on the original test sets, proving that our dictionaries and methods are not biased towards aligning word embeddings of proper nouns.

Non-English centric evaluation We analyze the performance of ID and ID++ for language pairs that do not include English. We use the test dictionaries from Vulić et al. (2019) that are derived from PanLex (Baldwin et al., 2010; Kamholz et al., 2014) by automatically translating each source language word into the target languages. We run VecMap for all combinations of Korean, Hebrew, and Thai. Romanized train lexicons are extracted by combining the languages through English (e.g., th-ko is obtained using en-th and en-ko), i.e., words are paired if their English translation is the same. Table 4 shows results. When Thai is involved, the unsupervised method fails as for English-Thai. Both ID and ID++ always outperform the respective unsupervised scores, and perform similar to higher-quality dictionaries. Additionally, ID++ outperforms ID in 3 out of 6 cases. These results demonstrate further the simplicity and high quality of our methods.

Romanized-only We analyze the performance of romanized pair lexicons on their own. Line Rom. in Table 2 and 3 shows that they obtain competitive results to the other two approaches, with improvements for Japanese, and perform similarly to MUSE dictionaries. The only failure is for Chinese (en-zh) – presumably because Chinese has a logographic script that does not represent phonemes directly, so romanization is less effective. These results show that the romanized pairs on their own also represent strong signals that shouldn't be neglected. Moreover, they constitute a good alternative when identical pairs are not available is such quantities (e.g., corpora of religious domain, law field, or cultural-specific documents).

Impact of OOVs We analyze the pairs used for the various sets (Appendix A, Table 5). We define OOVs as words for which there is no embedding available among the pre-trained Wikipedia fastText embeddings. Our romanized sets contain a substantial number of OOVs. (The identical pair sets do not contain OOVs because words are extracted from the top 200K most frequent.) The main reason for OOVs is that the selected English pair of a word is so rare that they do not have embeddings. On the other hand, the high number of OOVs (and resulting reduction of usable pairs) has only a limited negative impact on the performance.

Size of seed set and word frequency We analyze the impact of the size of the initial romanized seed set and of word frequency. Appendix A, Table 6, displays accuracy scores for MUSE and Romanized lexicons containing the $n \in \{25, 1000\}$ least and most frequent word pairs. Performance of VecMap applied to seed sets of size 25 is close to 0. The only exception is Russian, where the unsupervised approach already works well. Next, we investigate seed sets of size 1000 consisting of either the least frequent or the most frequent words. High-frequency seed sets give better results as expected. The effect is particularly strong for Tamil: the high-frequency set has performance close to the full set, whereas the low-frequency set is at $\leq$0.07. The performance of MUSE seed sets of size 25 and romanized seed sets of size 1000 is similar, demonstrating the higher quality of MUSE. However, obtaining the romanized pairs is much cheaper.

4. Conclusion

We have analyzed two cheap resources for building BWEs which can alleviate the issues of unsupervised methods which fail on multiple language pairs. We focused on a wide range of non-Latin languages paired with English. (i) We exploited identical pairs that surprisingly appear in corpora of distinct scripts. We showed that they can be used even when numerals are distinct in contrast to previous work. (ii) We combined them with a simple method to extract the initial hypothesis set via romanization and edit distance. With both approaches, we obtained results that are competitive with high-quality dictionaries. Without using explicit cross-lingual signal, we outperformed previous unsupervised work for most languages and in particular for five language pairs for which previous unsupervised work failed. Our results question the strong trend towards unsupervised mapping approaches, and show that cheap cross-lingual signals should always be considered for building BWEs, even for distant languages.

Acknowledgments

This work was funded by the European Research Council (grant #740516, #640550), the German Federal Ministry of Education and Research (BMBF, grant #01IS18036A), and the German Research Foundation (DFG; grant FR 2829/4-1).

5. Bibliographical References

Akbik, A., Blythe, D., and Vollgraf, R. (2018). Contextual string embeddings for sequence labeling. In *COLING 2018, 27th International Conference on Computational Linguistics*, pages 1638–1649.

Alaux, J., Grave, E., Cuturi, M., and Joulin, A. (2019). Unsupervised hyperalignment for multilingual word embeddings. In *Proceedings of the 7th International Conference on Learning Representations*.

Alvarez-Melis, D. and Jaakkola, T. S. (2018). Gromov-wasserstein alignment of word embedding spaces. In *EMNLP*.

Anzer, M., Chronopoulou, A., and Fraser, A. (2020). Comparing unsupervised and supervised approaches for kannada/english bilingual word embeddings. *Bachelor thesis at Ludwig Maximilians Universität München*.

Artetxe, M., Labaka, G., and Agirre, E. (2017). Learning bilingual word embeddings with (almost) no bilingual data. In *Proceedings of the 55th Annual Meeting of the Association for Computational Linguistics (Volume 1: Long Papers)*, pages 451–462.

Artetxe, M., Labaka, G., and Agirre, E. (2018). A robust self-learning method for fully unsupervised cross-lingual mappings of word embeddings. In *Proceedings of the 56th Annual Meeting of the Association for Computational Linguistics (Volume 1: Long Papers)*, pages 789–798.

Baldwin, T., Pool, J., and Colowick, S. (2010). Panlex and lextract: Translating all words of all languages of the world. In *Coling 2010: Demonstrations*, pages 37–40.

Chakravarthi, B. R., Arcan, M., and McCrae, J. P. (2019). Comparison of different orthographies for machine translation of under-resourced dravidian languages. In *2nd Conference on Language, Data and Knowledge (LDK 2019)*. Schloss Dagstuhl-Leibniz-Zentrum fuer Informatik.

Chen, X. and Cardie, C. (2018). Unsupervised multilingual word embeddings. *arXiv preprint arXiv:1808.08933*.

Dou, Z. Y., Zhou, Z. H., and Huang, S. (2020). Unsupervised bilingual lexicon induction via latent variable models. In *Proceedings of the 2018 Conference on Empirical Methods in Natural Language Processing*, pages 621–626.

Grave, E., Joulin, A., and Berthet, Q. (2019). Unsupervised alignment of embeddings with wasserstein procrustes. In *The 22nd International Conference on Artificial Intelligence and Statistics*, pages 1880–1890. PMLR.

Hoshen, Y. and Wolf, L. (2018). Non-adversarial unsupervised word translation. In *Proceedings of the 2018 Conference on Empirical Methods in Natural Language Processing*, pages 469–478.

Kamholz, D., Pool, J., and Colowick, S. (2014). Panlex: Building a resource for panlingual lexical translation. In *Proceedings of the Ninth International Conference on Language Resources and Evaluation (LREC'14)*, pages 3145–3150.

Kementchedjhieva, Y., Hartmann, M., and Søgaard, A. (2019). Lost in evaluation: Misleading benchmarks for bilingual dictionary induction. *arXiv preprint arXiv:1909.05708*.

Laville, M., Hazem, A., and Morin, E. (2020). Taln/ls2n participation at the bucc shared task: bilingual dictionary induction from comparable corpora. In *Proceedings of the 13th Workshop on Building and Using Comparable Corpora*, pages 56–60.

Levenshtein, V. I. (1966). Binary codes capable of correcting deletions, insertions, and reversals. *Soviet physics doklady*, 10(8):707–710.

Li, Y., Luo, Y., Lin, Y., Du, Q., Wang, H., Huang, S., Xiao, T., and Zhu, J. (2020). A simple and effective approach to robust unsupervised bilingual dictionary induction. In *Proceedings of the 28th International Conference on Computational Linguistics*, pages 5990–6001.

Marchisio, K., Duh, K., and Koehn, P. (2020). When does unsupervised machine translation work? *arXiv preprint arXiv:2004.05516*.

Mikolov, T., Le, Q. V., and Sutskever, I. (2013). Exploiting similarities among languages for machine translation. *arXiv preprint arXiv:1309.4168*.

Mohiuddin, T. and Joty, S. (2019). Revisiting adversarial autoencoder for unsupervised word translation with cycle consistency and improved training. In *Proceedings of NAACL-HLT*, pages 3857–3867.

Mohiuddin, M. T., Bari, M. S., and Joty, S. (2020). Lnmap: Departures from isomorphic assumption in bilingual lexicon induction through non-linear mapping in latent space. In *Proceedings of the 2020 Conference on Empirical Methods in Natural Language Processing (EMNLP)*, pages 2712–2723.

Riley, P. and Gildea, D. (2018). Orthographic features for bilingual lexicon induction. In *Proceedings of the 56th Annual Meeting of the Association for Computational Linguistics (Volume 2: Short Papers)*, pages 390–394.

Sabet, M. J., Dufter, P., Yvon, F., and Schütze, H. (2020). Simalign: High quality word alignments without parallel training data using static and contextualized embeddings. In *Findings of the Association for Computational Linguistics: EMNLP 2020*.

Severini, S., Hangya, V., Fraser, A., and Schütze, H. (2020a). Combining word embeddings with bilingual orthography embeddings for bilingual dictionary induction. In *Proceedings of the 28th International Conference on Computational Linguistics*, pages 6044–6055.

Severini, S., Hangya, V., Fraser, A., and Schütze, H. (2020b). Lmu bilingual dictionary induction system with word surface similarity scores for bucc 2020. In *Proceedings of the 13th Workshop on Building and Using Comparable Corpora*, pages 49–55.

Severini, S., Imani, A., Dufter, P., and Schütze, H. (2022). Towards a broad coverage named entity resource: A data-efficient approach for many diverse languages. *arXiv preprint arXiv:2201.12219*.

Smith, S. L., Turban, D. H., Hamblin, S., and Hammerla, N. Y. (2017). Offline bilingual word vectors, orthogonal transformations and the inverted softmax. *arXiv preprint arXiv:1702.03859*.

Søgaard, A., Ruder, S., and Vulić, I. (2018). On the limitations of unsupervised bilingual dictionary induction. In *Proceedings of the 56th Annual Meeting of the Association for Computational Linguistics (Volume 1: Long Papers)*, pages 778–788.

Vulić, I., Glavaš, G., Reichart, R., and Korhonen, A. (2019). Do we really need fully unsupervised cross-lingual embeddings? In *Proceedings of the 2019 Conference on Empirical Methods in Natural Language Processing and the 9th International Joint Conference on Natural Language Processing (EMNLP-IJCNLP)*, pages 4398–4409.

Zhang, M., Liu, Y., Luan, H., and Sun, M. (2017). Adversarial training for unsupervised bilingual lexicon induction. In *Proceedings of the 55th Annual Meeting of the Association for Computational Linguistics (Volume 1: Long Papers)*, pages 1959–1970.

6. Language Resource References

Bojanowski, P., Grave, E., Joulin, A., and Mikolov, T. (2017). Enriching Word Vectors with Subword Information. *Transactions of the Association for Computational Linguistics*, 5:135–146.

Hermjakob, U., May, J., and Knight, K. (2018). Out-of-the-box universal romanization tool uroman. In *Proceedings of ACL 2018, System Demonstrations*, pages 13–18.

Lample, G., Conneau, A., Ranzato, M., Denoyer, L., and Jégou, H. (2018). Word translation without parallel data. In *International Conference on Learning Representations*.

A. Statistics

In this section we show statistics on the language pairs analyzed and additional scores. Table 5 presents the number of pairs for each set that are not OOVs in the fastText wiki embeddings (Bojanowski et al., 2017) .

	MUSE	ID	Romanized	ID++
en-th	6,799	46,653	10,721 / 53,804	58779 / 101066
en-ja	7,135	43,556	11,488 / 118,626	54970 / 161848
en-kn	1,552	21,090	12,888 / 59,207	33843 / 80032
en-ta	8,091	23,538	5,987 / 120,836	29472 / 143990
en-zh	8,728	62,289	6,360 / 41,829	68597 / 103971
en-ar	11,571	19,275	4,773 / 61,031	24019 / 80115
en-hi	8,704	30,502	16,180 / 73,553	46557 / 103791
en-ru	10,887	18,663	9,913 / 301,698	28520 / 319688
en-el	10,662	35,270	20,740 / 150,472	55841 / 185244
en-fa	8,869	32,866	10,226 / 85,210	43019 / 117817
en-he	9,634	17,012	4,005 / 40,258	20977 / 57059
en-bn	8,467	31,954	10,721 / 53,804	42573 / 85532
en-ko	7,999	15,518	9956 / 134156	25344 / 149031

Table 5: Number of pairs used that are not OOVs in the fastText wiki embeddings compared to the full size of the sets. For MUSE full and identical pairs sets there are no OOVs.

B. Main results

In Table 7 there are the accuracy scores based on CSLS vector similarity calculated by the MUSE evaluation tool (Lample et al., 2018). We show the scores for thirteen language pairs in both directions. The first five pairs are the ones for which unsupervised methods fail. We show both unsupervised and semi-supervised VecMap performance with baselines dictionaries and our three sets.

C. MUSE proper nouns removal

Table 8 shows results computed on the subsets of MUSE test sets that don't contain proper nouns. We remove proper nouns using the list of names obtained in Section 2.2 The new sets contains 10% less pairs on average.

D. Reproducibility

We run our method on up to 48 cores of Intel(R) Xeon(R) CPU E7-8857 v2 with 1TB memory and a single GeForce GTX 1080 GPU with 8GB memory. The training of semi-suprised BWEs using VecMap took approximately 1 hour per language pair. For VecMap, as well as for all others methods we analyzed, we used the latest code available in their git repositories with default parameters. ID++ is implemented in Python.

		MUSE				Rom.			
		25L	25H	1000L	1000H	25L	25H	1000L	1000H
en-ta	→	14.73	16.27	17.33	17.40	0.00	0.00	0.07	17.80
	←	16.48	18.35	22.44	23.44	0.00	0.00	0.00	21.57
en-fa	→	35.33	34.20	38.07	37.20	0.00	0.20	37.47	37.47
	←	41.73	42.60	44.14	44.21	0.07	0.13	42.40	43.40
en-zh	→	39.00	39.40	38.20	37.67	0.00	0.00	0.07	0.40
	←	32.93	34.47	34.33	34.40	0.00	0.00	0.07	0.60
en-ru	→	49.07	43.07	49.07	49.27	49.33	47.73	49.40	49.00
	←	65.93	60.60	65.93	66.13	65.80	64.47	65.60	66.40

Table 6: acc@1 using 25 or 1000 pairs lower-frequency (L) and higher-frequency (H) sets for MUSE and our romanized only (Rom.) set.

			Baselines				Our		
			Unsupervised			Semi-sup.	Semi-sup.		
			1	2	3	MUSE	ID	Rom.	ID++
1	en-th	→	0.00	0.00	0.00	**24.33**	**24.40**	23.33	23.47
		←	0.00	0.00	0.00	**19.04**	**19.92**	17.96	19.85
2	en-ja	→	0.96	0.48	0.00	**48.73**	48.87	48.46	**49.14**
		←	0.96	0.00	0.00	**32.87**	33.22	**34.80**	33.43
3	en-kn	→	0.00	0.00	0.00	**23.78***	22.03	22.90	**24.23**
		←	0.00	0.00	0.00	**41.25***	**43.04**	42.50	41.79
4	en-ta	→	0.07	0.07	0.00$^{\diamond}$	**18.80**	17.93	18.00	**18.20**
		←	0.07	0.00	0.00$^{\diamond}$	**24.38**	**24.78**	23.51	**24.78**
5	en-zh	→	0.07	0.00	0.00	**36.53**	**37.00**	0.27	35.00
		←	0.00	0.00	0.00	**32.80**	**34.33**	0.07	32.67
6	en-ar	→	33.60	7.67	36.30$^{\diamond}$	**39.87**	**40.27**	39.33	40.20
		←	47.72	12.92	52.60$^{\diamond}$	**54.48**	54.42	54.42	**54.62**
7	en-hi	→	40.20	0.00	0.00$^{\diamond}$	**40.33**	**40.47**	39.60	40.20
		←	**50.57**	0.07	0.00$^{\diamond}$	50.50	49.77	49.90	**50.10**
8	en-ru	→	**48.80**	37.33	46.90$^{\diamond}$	**48.80**	49.13	48.87	**49.53**
		←	**66.13**	52.73	64.70$^{\diamond}$	65.67	**66.13**	65.73	66.07
9	en-el	→	47.67	34.67	47.90$^{\diamond}$	**48.00**	47.87	48.00	**48.27**
		←	63.40	49.20	**63.50**$^{\diamond}$	63.33	63.27	**64.40**	63.47
10	en-fa	→	33.27	0.53	36.70$^{\diamond}$	**38.00**	**37.67**	36.80	**37.67**
		←	39.99	0.40	**44.50**$^{\diamond}$	43.47	**43.67**	42.93	43.60
11	en-he	→	44.60	37.13	44.00$^{\diamond}$	**45.00**	44.47	44.53	**44.67**
		←	57.88	50.01	57.10$^{\diamond}$	**57.94**	**58.14**	57.81	57.94
12	en-bn	→	18.20	0.00	0.00$^{\diamond}$	**21.60**	19.87	19.80	**20.13**
		←	22.19	0.00	0.00$^{\diamond}$	**28.46**	28.88	28.67	**29.41**
13	en-ko	→	19.80	9.62	0.00	**28.94**	27.92	28.40	**28.81**
		←	24.37	13.83	0.00	**34.09**	33.40	33.74	**33.95**

Table 7: acc@1 for unsupervised methods (1: Artetxe et al. (2018), 2: Grave et al. (2019), 3: Mohiuddin and Joty (2019)) and semi-supervised VecMap with different initial lexicons: MUSE set, identical pairs dataset (ID), our romanized only sets (Rom.), and the union of identical and romanized pairs (ID++). We show both forward (→) and backward (←) directions. In bold the best result for each pair of languages, for "Baselines" and "Our". Scores from Mohiuddin et al. (2020) are marked with $^{\diamond}$.
*Kannada is not supported by MUSE, so we use the dictionary provided by (Anzer et al., 2020).

			Baselines		Our		
			Unsup	Semi-sup. MUSE	Semi-supervised ID	Rom.	ID++
1	en-th	→	0.00	**27.21**	**27.13**	26.35	26.11
		←	0.00	18.93	19.83	18.25	19.83
2	en-ja	→	0.71	**46.15**	45.04	46.31	**46.39**
		←	0.56	**39.14**	38.86	**40.73**	39.52
3	en-kn	→	0.00	**23.78***	22.03	22.90	**24.23**
		←	0.00	**41.25***	**43.04**	42.50	41.79
4	en-ta	→	0.08	**20.12**	19.35	18.97	**19.43**
		←	0.08	**24.60**	24.60	23.71	**25.00**
5	en-zh	→	0.07	**37.34**	**38.14**	0.07	35.74
		←	0.00	**32.48**	**34.83**	0.00	32.48
6	en-ar	→	35.44	**39.70**	**40.23**	39.24	40.15
		←	49.75	**53.61**	53.46	53.61	**53.82**
7	en-hi	→	**42.49**	42.42	**42.79**	42.11	42.57
		←	52.46	**52.62**	51.99	52.07	**52.23**
8	en-ru	→	**45.64**	**45.64**	46.40	45.64	**46.70**
		←	**64.35**	64.13	64.57	64.35	**64.72**
9	en-el	→	48.90	**49.35**	48.97	49.43	**49.58**
		←	**63.87**	63.80	63.87	**64.56**	63.72
10	en-fa	→	34.18	**37.51**	37.35	36.58	**37.59**
		←	41.78	**43.59**	**44.06**	43.35	43.82
11	en-he	→	42.22	**42.60**	**42.29**	42.14	**42.29**
		←	**55.92**	55.70	56.00	55.62	**56.08**
12	en-bn	→	20.44	**22.74**	21.59	20.52	**20.98**
		←	25.80	**30.22**	30.30	30.30	**30.96**
13	en-ko	→	20.30	**26.57**	25.63	26.02	**26.49**
		←	26.52	**32.37**	**32.21**	31.80	32.13

Table 8: acc@1 on MUSE test sets without proper nouns. Results are reported for unsupervised and semi-supervised Vecmap Artetxe et al. (2018) with different initial lexicons: MUSE set, identical pairs dataset (ID), our romanized only sets (Rom.), and the union of identical and romanized pairs (ID++). We show both forward (→) and backward (←) directions. In bold the best result for each pair of languages, for "Baselines" and "Our".
*Kannada is not supported by MUSE, so we use the dictionary provided by (Anzer et al., 2020).

Proceedings of the 15th Workshop on Building and Using Comparable Corpora (BUCC 2022) @LREC2022 , pages 23–32
Marseille, June 25, 2022
© European Language Resources Association (ELRA), licensed under CC-BY-NC

Building Domain-specific Corpora from the Web: the Case of European Digital Service Infrastructures

Rik van Noord[1], Cristian García-Romero[2], Miquel Esplà-Gomis[2]
Leopoldo Pla[2], Antonio Toral[1]
[1]University of Groningen, [2]Universitat d'Alacant
rikvannoord@gmail.com, cgarcia@dlsi.ua.es
mespla@dlsi.ua.es, lpla@dlsi.ua.es, a.toral.ruiz@rug.nl

Abstract

An important goal of the MaCoCu project is to improve EU-specific NLP systems that concern their Digital Service Infrastructures (DSIs). In this paper we aim at boosting the creation of such domain-specific NLP systems. To do so, we explore the feasibility of building an automatic classifier that allows to identify which segments in a generic (potentially parallel) corpus are relevant for a particular DSI. We create an evaluation data set by crawling DSI-specific web domains and then compare different strategies to build our DSI classifier for text in three languages: English, Spanish and Dutch. We use pre-trained (multilingual) language models to perform the classification, with zero-shot classification for Spanish and Dutch. The results are promising, as we are able to classify DSIs with between 70 and 80% accuracy, even without in-language training data. A manual annotation of the data revealed that we can also find DSI-specific data on crawled texts from general web domains with reasonable accuracy. We publicly release all data, predictions and code, as to allow future investigations in whether exploiting this DSI-specific data actually leads to improved performance on particular applications, such as machine translation.

Keywords: Digital Service Infrastructures, Text Classification, Web Crawling

1. Introduction

The Connecting Europe Facility (CEF)[1] was set up by the European Commission to promote growth, jobs and competitiveness through targeted infrastructure investment at the European level. A key component is the e-Translation platform[2] of the European Language Resource Coordination program, which provides automated translation to facilitate multilingual communication and exchange of documents between public administrations and citizens of the EU and CEF-affiliated countries. A main application of this platform is on their services called *Digital Service Infrastructures* (henceforth DSIs, see Table 1 for an overview). For these services to function adequately, it is of vital importance that the automatic translations of texts and documents are of high quality.

Among DSIs, it is easy to identify clearly different textual domains, such as information technologies, health systems, legal processes, etc. On the other hand, they are also complex, compartmentalized and often highly specific, making it challenging, for example, to train a single machine translation (MT) model that would perform well across all DSIs. It would clearly be beneficial to use domain-specific MT systems for different areas and domains, rather than using a single generic MT system for all of them. We therefore work under the hypothesis that the MT used within the scope of each DSI can be improved by carefully selecting relevant training data per individual DSI, rather than simply using generic training data. Common methods to exploit such data include pre-training on generic data and fine-tuning on domain-specific data (Luong and Manning, 2015; Freitag and Al-Onaizan, 2016), instance weighting (Wang et al., 2017) and pivot-based domain adaptation (Li et al., 2018; Ben-David et al., 2020). In order to obtain this domain-specific data, we would require an automatic system that can classify sentences into whether they fit in a DSI or not. To the best of our knowledge, no such system exists yet. Therefore, in this paper, we aim at building such a DSI classifier as a first step in potentially creating DSI-specific MT systems. Given the multilingual nature of Europe and the DSIs, we will attempt to build a classifier that can handle multiple languages. To achieve this, we first crawl DSI-specific websites, whose content will then be used to train our automatic classifier.

Our ultimate goal, as part of the MaCoCu project[3], is to apply this classifier to generic web-crawled corpora in official EU (or related) languages, such as ParaCrawl (Bañón et al., 2020a).[4] We will not release hard categories per sentence or document, but rather release the softmax probability distribution of our best model over the DSI categories.[5] Users can then simply select their own threshold in selecting instances per DSI. Since most of these corpora are parallel with English, only having an English parser could suffice, but we would also want to be able to classify non-parallel corpora for non-English languages. Therefore, we will also train

[1]`https://ec.europa.eu/inea/en/connecting-europe-facility`

[2]`https://webgate.ec.europa.eu/etranslation/public/welcome.html`

[3]`https://macocu.eu/`

[4]`https://www.paracrawl.eu/`

[5]Though note that not all DSIs are necessarily completely disjoint classes (see Section 2).

		English		Spanish		Dutch	
DSI	**Domain**	Crawled	Clean	Crawled	Clean	Crawled	Clean
BRIS	Business, Market	0	0	0	0	0	0
Cybersecurity	ICT	1,390,239	209,053	176,886	40,425	5,237	759
EESSI	Social security	267,086	49,345	30,181	2,398	5,979	739
E-health	Health, Medicine	63,582	13,891	75	31	0	0
E-justice	Justice, Law	6,942,090	262,933	2,277,413	146,968	1,356,537	151,752
E-procurement	Public procurement	23,133	3,557	0	0	0	0
Europeana	Culture	965,220	14,327	76,037	1,566	0	0
ODR	Consumers' rights	4,669,948	163,365	3,849,469	104,251	101,704	20,842
Open Data Portal	Multiple domains	33,792,223	75,394	254	19	703	228
Safer Internet	ICT	134,439	24,767	142	39	125	9

Table 1: The number of crawled and cleaned sentences per DSI, per language.

a multilingual model on the English data, that is able to perform zero-shot classification. We will test our method on Spanish and Dutch, aside from English, as these languages are MaCoCu objectives. Though we look in particular at DSIs, we believe this paper can be beneficial to all researchers that are interested in classifying web-crawled data for specific textual domains. A description of the crawling of DSI-specific data is provided in Section 2, after which we evaluate the performance of our DSI classifiers in Section 3. Our English and Spanish classifiers perform quite well, with Dutch lagging a bit behind. We obtain the best DSI classification performance by fine-tuning a pretrained language model, with DEBERTA for English and XLM-R for Spanish and Dutch. We then apply the best English model on two corpora of unseen ParaCrawl sentences in Section 4 and analyse its performance by manually annotating a subset of the data.

2. Data

DSIs The targeted DSIs (listed in Table 1, taken from the MaCoCu project) range from rather general (E-health, Cybersecurity) to highly specific, such as Electronic Exchange of Social Security Information (EESSI) and the Business Registers Interconnection System (BRIS). Even looking at just the DSIs themselves, and the corresponding textual domains, shows that this task will be challenging. First, there is considerable overlap between the domain of some DSIs, namely for Cybersecurity & Safer Internet and for E-justice & Online Dispute Resolution (ODR).[6] Moreover, there are also DSIs that are very general and hard to define exactly in terms of domain (e.g. Europeana, Open Data Portal).

ELRC-Share There already exists a database with corpora that are tagged with certain DSIs: ELRC-Share (Lösch et al., 2018). However, on a closer inspection we found that it did not match our exact needs. First, many of the corpora are tagged with all DSIs, but do not actually assign a DSI per sentence, document or any subset of the corpus. The tags only seem to indicate that the corpus *could* be useful when working with DSI data. Second, the DSI tags often seem questionable or plain wrong. For example, there are a number of corpora tagged with *Europeana* that contain just general texts (news, Wikipedia) and are not specific to the *Culture* domain (see Table 1). Third, the correctly tagged corpora usually contain little data or are highly specific, likely making it difficult to train a general classifier on it. Fourth, even if there is data available, it is mainly for English, with very sparse resources for other languages. For these reasons, we decided to crawl our own DSI-specific data. We will outline this process below.

2.1. Crawling DSI-specific web domains

First, we create a methodology to select the DSI-specific web domains we will crawl. For some DSIs there was only a single domain publicly available (e.g. *Europeana*). In the case of the DSIs that do not have a specific portal, we manually checked the publicly available information about projects related to these DSIs.[7] We also used Google results to obtain more web domains. Finally, we selected the official website of the European Commission[8], since it contains data relevant for some DSIs, though in the end we only found data for *EESSI* (`ec.europa.eu/social`). Note that for certain DSIs, the whole service consists of more than what can be found on a website, for example software packages for *Cybersecurity*. The full list of domains crawled per DSI can be found in Appendix C.

Once we selected all the web domains for the DSIs with services available on a website, we used Bitextor[9] in order to crawl them and process the result-

[6]However, throughout the paper, we do treat them as separate categories.

[7]`https://ec.europa.eu/inea/en/connecting-europe-facility/cef-telecom/projects-by-dsi`

[8]`https://ec.europa.eu`

[9]`https://github.com/bitextor/bitextor`

	English			Spanish		Dutch	
DSI	Train	Dev.	Test	Dev.	Test	Dev.	Test
Cybersecurity	207,053	1,000	1,000	1,000	1,000	379	380
EESSI	47,345	1,000	1,000	1,000	1,000	369	370
E-health	11,891	1,000	1,000	0	0	0	0
E-justice	260,933	1,000	1,000	1,000	1,000	1,000	1,000
Europeana	12,327	1,000	1,000	783	783	0	0
Online Dispute Resolution	161,365	1,000	1,000	1,000	1,000	1,000	1,000
Open Data Portal	73,394	1,000	1,000	0	0	114	114
Safer Internet	22,767	1,000	1,000	0	0	0	0
Other	797,075	8,000	8,000	4,783	4,783	2,862	2,864
Total	1,594,150	16,000	16,000	9,566	9,566	5,724	5,728

Table 2: Label division for the sentence-level train, development and test sets for the three languages of interest.

ing data.[10] Bitextor is a tool to harvest bitexts from multilingual websites, but in this case we have just used the first part of the pipeline, which is a monolingual process. For crawling, we use `wget` and store the data downloaded in the Web ARChive (WARC) file format..[11] Then, WARC files are processed using `warc2preprocess`, which involves:

1. Applying the Fix Text For You library (FTFY) (Speer, 2019) to fix common text problems such as *mojibake* (that is, garbled text that is the result of text being decoded using an unintended character encoding).
2. Detecting the language of the documents with CLD2[12] and discarding those which are not in one of the targeted languages.
3. Removing boilerplates (that is, text which is the same from page to page, usually menu items or footer elements) using Boilerpipe (Kohlschütter et al., 2010).
4. Parsing HTML using the HTML tokenizer implemented in the Python code of `warc2preprocess` in Bitextor, which takes into account the structure of the HTML elements for a more accurate paragraph and segment delimitation when extracting plain text.

We apply a number of cleaning steps to the extracted texts after the 4 previously described steps of the WARC process. First, we split the text into sentences using the Moses sentence splitter (Koehn et al., 2007) and normalize quotes, dashes and other punctuation. Then, we tokenize the sentences using SpaCy[13] and only keep those with more than 6 and less than 50 tokens. This is the step where we lose the majority of the crawled sentences, as the crawls often contain short texts that are likely headers, links or menu options which are not filtered out by Boilerpipe. Finally, we filter out sentences that are (near)-duplicates, sentences that do not end with punctuation and sentences that are classified as a different language according to CLD3.[14] In Table 1, *Clean* shows the number of sentences per DSI, per language that are left after this final cleaning process. Multiple authors carried out a manual inspection on a sample of the cleaned data, which confirmed that the data was of high quality and relevant for the selected DSIs, according to our criteria.

2.2. Splits

We did not find sufficient training data for all DSI-language pairs. For English, we do not train and evaluate on BRIS and E-procurement. For Dutch and Spanish we do not need training data (since we perform zero-shot classification), but even so we only find sufficient data in 5 out of 10 DSIs (see Table 2). For each DSI, we take (at most) 1,000 sentences for the development and test set. We split the data sequentially, e.g. the first 11,891 crawled sentences of *E-health* are put in the training set, while the last 2,000 are put in the dev and test set, respectively. We do this to minimize train-test overlap: this way, sentences from the same webpage will not occur in both train and test. We did experiment with random splitting (where this overlap would be possible) and found higher F_1-scores, indicating that this indeed had an effect.

We also want our model to be able to recognize sentences that do not belong to any of the DSIs. To this end, we introduce the *Other* category, which consists of random sentences taken from Paracrawl (Bañón et al., 2020b) release v9. For English, the sentences are taken from the parallel side of the Spanish and Dutch releases. We actually expect that most of the randomly

[10]See Figure 4 in Appendix A for exact settings.

[11]`https://iipc.github.io/warc-specifications/specifications/warc-format/warc-1.1/`

[12]`https://github.com/CLD2Owners/cld2`

[13]`https://spacy.io/`

[14]CLD2 was used only at the document level, as it can parse HTML and detect language of text blocks; CLD3 was used at the segment level for robustness, as it is more accurate than CLD2 but cannot be used on HTML documents.

crawled sentences would fit this non-DSI category best (and our analyses in Section 4 seem to confirm this). To strike a balance between mimicking this expected distribution and enabling the model to learn about DSIs specifically, we ensure that half of the training, development and test set sentences belong to this category. An important thing to note about this *Other* category is that it might contain instances that could well belong to a DSI. In other words: predicting a DSI instead of *Other* is not necessarily a mistake, though we do treat it as such throughout the paper.

Down-sampling Our training set distribution is quite different from that of the development and test sets. Therefore, it is likely that it is suboptimal (or at least inefficient) to maintain all training instances during training. We experiment with *down-sampling* the majority categories during training, i.e. randomly selecting a subset of instances per DSI. Importantly, the *Other* category gets a special treatment: we ensure it is always the same size as the DSI-instances combined (similar as the initial division in Table 2). As an example, down-sampling to 10,000 sentences per DSI means a total training set of 80,000 + 80,000 = 160,000 instances.

3. Experiments

This section outlines our experimental setup and experiments we performed. All code to reproduce our results is publicly available at: `https://github.com/RikVN/DSI`

Baseline As a baseline system, we use a simple bag-of-words support vector machine (SVM) model implemented using scikit-learn (Pedregosa et al., 2011). Our best baseline model is a linear SVM that uses unigrams and bigrams with a tf-idf vectorizer. Each feature has to occur at least five times (regardless of corpus size) to be included and we use a C-value of 1. Other settings are left at default.

Language models Our main classification method is fine-tuning a pretrained (multilingual) neural language model (LM). We use the (de facto) default method of fine-tuning such an LM: adding a single classification layer (with dropout) on top of the pooled layers, as implemented in the `transformers` library of Huggingface (Wolf et al., 2020). To determine which pretrained LM is the most suitable for our task, we experiment with quite a number of LMs that are well-established in the literature. For English, we experiment with BART (Lewis et al., 2020), BERT (Devlin et al., 2019), CANINE (Clark et al., 2021), DEBERTA (He et al., 2021), ELECTRA (Clark et al., 2020), Longformer (Beltagy et al., 2020), ROBERTA (Liu et al., 2019), XLM-en (Conneau et al., 2020) and XLNET (Yang et al., 2019), while for the zero-shot experiments for Spanish and Dutch we experiment with M-BART, M-BERT, M-DEBERTA and XLM-R. For models that have a base and large variant available, we experimented only with the large models. We apply temperature scaling (Guo et al., 2017) to ensure a better probability distribution in the final classification layer. We select the best models in Section 3.1.

	Acc.	Prec.	Rec.	F_1
BART-large	77.3	67.7	65.3	65.9
BERT-large	75.8	66.1	63.3	64.0
CANINE	68.8	56.6	54.0	54.9
DEBERTA-v3-large	**77.5**	**68.1**	**66.1**	**66.4**
ELECTRA-large	74.4	64.3	61.7	62.3
Longformer-large	76.3	67.0	63.9	64.7
ROBERTA-large	75.8	66.3	63.2	64.1
XLM-en	65.1	52.6	50.5	51.0
XLNET-large	77.0	67.9	65.3	66.1

Table 3: Development set results (all in %) for English DSI-classification for a number of pretrained LMs. Precision, recall and F_1-score are macro-averaged.

Evaluation As stated previously, we ultimately intend to release probability distributions of the classifier. However, for evaluation purposes, we still evaluate our models by using hard classification (i.e. by taking the argmax of the probability distribution). For each experiment we report both the accuracy as well the macro-averaged precision, recall and F_1-score. Numbers are single runs, unless otherwise indicated.

3.1. English DSI classification

First, we try to find the LM that is most suitable for this task. For efficiency reasons we perform these experiments on a subset of our data set: down-sampling each DSI-category to 3,000 instances and therefore using 24,000 instances for *Other* (see last paragraph of Section 2.2). The development and test sets are not changed. For each LM, we tune the learning rate, as the default learning rate is often far from optimal. The results of this experiment are reported in Table 3.

We take the best performing system (DEBERTA-large) and tune the other hyper-parameters. Specifically, we experiment with warm-up ratio, label smoothing, dropout, batch size and gradient clipping (see Appendix B for best settings and range of values tried). Our best performing system obtained an accuracy and F_1-score of 77.5% and 66.4%, respectively. We also experimented with freezing the LM layers and only training the classification layer, but this did not lead to improved performance.

3.2. Zero-shot DSI classification

We also perform zero-shot multilingual DSI classification by fine-tuning pretrained multilingual language models (MLMs). We train only on the English data set, and test on the Spanish and Dutch sets. We apply similar steps as for the English language models: we experiment with different pre-trained MLMs, for which we only tune the learning rate. The other hyperparameters are set to the best values we found in the English experiments. Note that for both Spanish and Dutch, this is only 6-class classification, as opposed to

	Spanish				Dutch			
	Acc	P	R	F_1	Acc	P	R	F_1
M-BART	73.5	**77.7**	58.5	64.4	63.5	52.1	47.4	46.5
M-BERT	70.8	70.6	56.5	61.3	60.7	42.0	42.2	40.6
M-DEBERTA	74.3	74.5	63.6	68.0	62.8	54.8	49.7	48.4
XLM-R	**76.1**	77.4	**65.4**	**70.5**	**64.9**	**55.4**	**53.2**	**50.8**

Table 4: Development set results (all in %) for zero-shot DSI-classification for Spanish and Dutch. Precision (P), recall (R), and F_1 score are macro-averaged.

the 9-class classification task for English. The results are shown in Table 4. We find that XLM-R is the best model for both languages, though the difference with M-DEBERTA is modest. Generally, we find the scores to be promising, given that it is a zero-shot multi-class classification. Interestingly, the best Spanish model obtains higher F_1-scores than the best English model, though the task is also somewhat easier since Spanish only has six classes. Moreover, Spanish has no data for *Open Data Portal*, which was the hardest DSI for the English model (see Appendix D).

3.3. Down-sampling ratio

Previous experiments were performed using down-sampled data sets of at most 3,000 instances per DSI in the training set. To get the best performance, we aim to find the optimal down-sampling size for the best model per language. We plot the performance in Figure 1. Interestingly, even the LMs still benefit from large amounts of extra data, though the differences are modest. Best performance for the models is obtained for down-sampling the categories to between $20,000$ and $50,000$ instances. Note that all models were tested for $> 50,000$ instances, but always decreased in performance. For each language, we select the best model and evaluate on the test set. These scores are shown in Table 5. For English and Spanish, the model performs quite well, with accuracies around 80%. Interestingly,

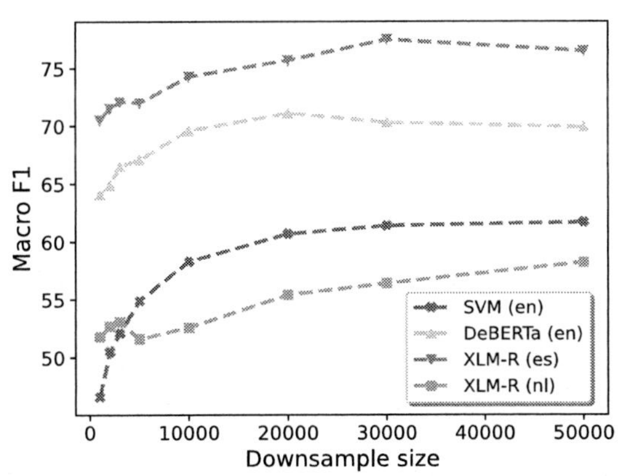

Figure 1: Dev set macro F_1 scores (in %) per down-sampled size per category for the different languages.

		Acc.	Prec.	Rec.	F_1
EN	Dev.	79.8 ± 0.6	73.7 ± 0.7	68.6 ± 1.7	70.4 ± 0.7
	Test	77.3 ± 0.3	71.6 ± 0.9	64.4 ± 1.1	67.1 ± 0.3
ES	Dev.	81.2 ± 0.4	81.3 ± 0.9	74.5 ± 0.7	77.5 ± 0.4
	Test	80.2 ± 0.2	80.0 ± 0.8	72.7 ± 0.7	75.9 ± 0.3
NL	Dev.	70.9 ± 1.0	61.2 ± 1.3	63.0 ± 1.4	57.9 ± 0.8
	Test	74.1 ± 1.1	67.0 ± 1.2	65.2 ± 0.8	62.8 ± 0.5

Table 5: Final development and test set scores (in %) of our best model per language. Results are averaged over three runs. Note that since we calculate the macro average, F_1 is not necessarily between *Prec.* and *Rec.*

the scores for Dutch actually increase on the test set. The detailed scores per DSI are shown in Appendix D. The hardest DSI to classify for the English model is *Open Data Portal*. This is not unexpected; as we noted previously, this is a very broad DSI that consists of multiple domains (see Table 1). The model does quite well on *Other*, which is likely due to it being the majority class, but also on *Europeana*. We hypothesize that this is due to *Europeana* being the most dissimilar DSI, as compared to the other DSIs, since it is not related to any legal or digital EU domains.

It is interesting to observe which categories are most difficult to distinguish for the model. The confusion matrix of our best English model is shown in Figure 2. Curiously, Cybersecurity and Safer Internet are actually not confused often, even though they are both in the ICT domain. Cybersecurity is, however, the most common wrong prediction for E-justice, which is also surprising, as the two do not seem directly related. Lastly, *Open Data Portal* seems to be a very broad DSI, since it is confused with a lot of different DSIs.

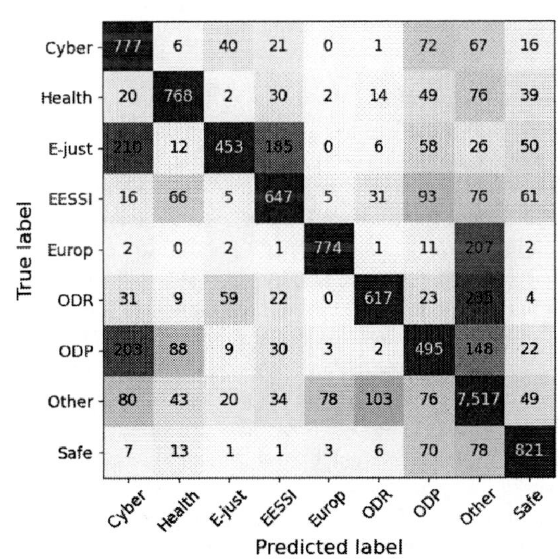

Figure 2: Confusion matrix of development set performance of our best English model.

	Dutch-English					Spanish-English				
	>0.3	**>0.5**	**>0.7**	**>0.8**	**>0.9**	**>0.3**	**>0.5**	**>0.7**	**>0.8**	**>0.9**
Cybersecurity	1.1	0.8	0.6	0.5	0.3	1.3	1.0	0.8	0.7	0.4
EESSI	0.7	0.5	0.4	0.3	0.1	0.7	0.6	0.4	0.3	0.1
E-health	0.9	0.5	0.3	0.2	0.1	0.8	0.4	0.3	0.2	0.1
E-justice	0.6	0.5	0.4	0.3	0.1	0.6	0.5	0.4	0.3	0.1
Europeana	2.1	1.7	1.4	1.3	0.6	2.2	1.8	1.5	1.3	0.6
Online Dispute Resolution	3.0	2.5	2.1	1.8	1.2	3.3	2.7	2.3	2.0	1.3
Open Data Portal	0.6	0.5	0.4	0.3	0.2	0.7	0.6	0.5	0.4	0.2
Safer Internet	0.4	0.3	0.3	0.2	0.1	0.6	0.5	0.4	0.3	0.2
Other	90.7	90.0	89.1	88.2	82.9	89.9	89.1	88.2	87.3	82.1

Table 6: Percentage of total instances per DSI per softmax threshold, when classifying 89 million and 269 million sentences for the English-Dutch and English-Spanish ParaCrawl releases with our best English model. Note that the columns do not necessarily sum to 100%.

4. Analysis

Classifying unseen data The ultimate goal of our system is to classify previously unseen generic web-crawled data. To get a sense of how many DSI-specific instances we can find in such randomly crawled data, we use our best English model to classify the English sentences from the latest Dutch-English and Spanish-English ParaCrawl releases, consisting of 89 million and 269 million sentences, respectively.[15] Note that since we used this data also to create the *Other* category, we actually train two models to ensure the model that is used never saw any of the ParaCrawl data as *Other* during training. The results for using different softmax thresholds are shown in Table 6. As expected, the vast majority of the data does not get classified as belonging to a specific DSI. Around 8% of the sentences get classified as a DSI for a softmax threshold value > 0.5, which quickly decreases for higher values. Though small, this is not necessarily a problem, since there are billions of English sentences publicly available, potentially allowing us to still create large corpora per DSI for this language.

Manual annotation However, this method will only work well if the predictions on unseen data are of reasonable quality. To evaluate this, we asked an expert annotator to manually annotate 800 of the ParaCrawl predictions, 100 for each DSI. We asked the annotator: *Does this sentence fit in DSI X*? For 400 sentences, X is actually the predicted DSI by our best English model. In the other 400, the DSI is chosen randomly. This lets us compare how meaningful the predicted DSIs are, without having to annotate from scratch, which greatly speeds up the process. We do not annotate *Other*, as this is meaningless: all sentences potentially fit this DSI, so annotators by definition should always answer "yes" to whether the sentence fits this category.

The results are shown in Table 7, and are mostly reassuring. As an example, let us look at the DSI *Cybersecurity*. For the 100 instances the model predicted this DSI, the annotator was asked 50 times whether the sentences actually belonged in *Cybersecurity*, answering "yes" in 50% of those instances. For the other 50, the annotator was asked whether the sentence belonged to a randomly selected different DSI. Of those 50, only 10% of the sentences were accepted as belonging to that DSI. We found similar results for all DSIs, as on average, predicted DSIs by the model are about 5 times as likely to fit that DSI than randomly selected DSIs. On the other hand, for 4 out of 8 DSIs less than half of the predictions are actually annotated to fit the respective DSI (first column of results).

Model confidence We can now also analyse the importance of the softmax probability (i.e. the confidence) of the model. In other words: does the model get more accurate as it gets more confident? For 400 annotations, where X was the predicted DSI, we now know whether the model made a fitting prediction. For the other 400, answering "no" during the annotation process does not tell us if the prediction of the model was correct, only that the randomly picked DSI was incorrect. Using the former 400 instances, we plot the accuracy of the model over minimum confidence val-

	Pred. (%)	**Random (%)**
Cybersecurity	50.0	10.0
EESSI	42.0	10.0
E-health	44.0	12.0
E-justice	78.0	8.0
Europeana	88.0	2.0
ODR	54.0	14.0
Open Data Portal	36.0	14.0
Safer Internet	66.0	20.0
Total	57.2	11.2

Table 7: Percentage of "yes" annotations per DSI. **Pred** means the model actually predicted this DSI, while **Random** means we picked a random DSI to annotate for the respective sentence.

[15] Predictions available at `https://macocu.eu`

DSI	Type	Best features
Cybersecurity	All	enisa, cybersecurity, concordia, cert, nis, cyber, vulnerability, attacker
	Word	cert, nis, vulnerability, attacker, vulnerabilities, security, attackers, the agency
EESSI	All	eures, egf, fead, easi, administrative commission, movers, social partners, etuc
	Word	administrative commission, movers, social partners, posting industrial relations, apprenticeships, vet, workers
E-health	All	ehtel, digitalhealtheurope, twinning, ehealth, mhealth, digital health, dhe, telemedicine
	Word	twinning, digital health, health data, twinnings, healthcare, scirocco, patient, health
E-justice	All	eurojust, ccbe, jits, jit, ocg, isil, lawyers, videoconferencing
	Word	lawyers, debtor, court, creditors, judicial, this treaty, prosecutor, casework
Europeana	All	europeana, beavers, beaver, lindgren, hotjar, simberg, this gallery, merian
	Word	beavers, beaver, this gallery, curie, kimono, counterculture, digital object, rights statement
ODR	All	eni, fastweb, sncf, amf, riai, cssf, cru, ecogra
	Word	cru, uke, issuers, lithuania, management company, irish water, nais, state legal
Open Data Portal	All	open data, psi, datasets, technical purpose, dataset, edp, portals, re users
	Word	open data, psi, datasets, technical purpose, dataset, edp, portals, re users
Safer-internet	All	inhope, csam, hotline, bik, hotlines, sic, helpline, aviator
	Word	hotline, sic, aviator, better internet, bee secure, sid, media literacy, young people
Other	All	your, the, you, god, triodos, is, click, hotel
	Word	your, the, you, god, is, click, hotel, reserves the

Table 8: Most important SVM-features per DSI for English DSI classification. The row "word" shows the 8 best features that are also English words.

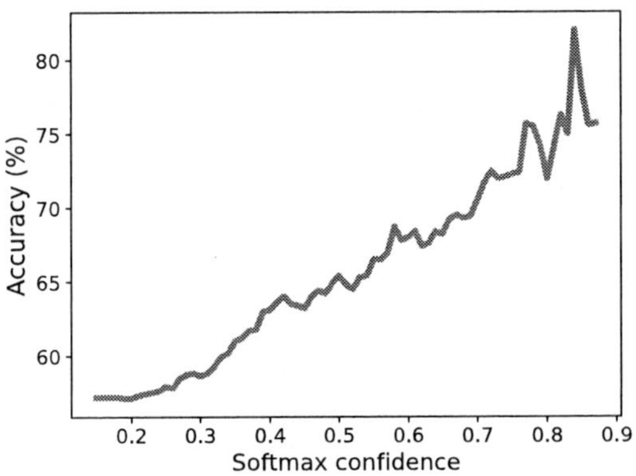

Figure 3: Accuracy of the best English model for 400 annotated instances, with a minimum confidence.

ues in Figure 3, with a confidence of 0.15 including all 400 instances, while a confidence of 0.85 only includes 50. This gives us a clear answer to our question: the model indeed gets more accurate as it gets more confident. This means that it is possible for users to determine their own data/quality trade-off, with higher softmax thresholds leading to fewer data that is of higher quality. It is hard for us to suggest an optimal threshold value, as it will likely differ per task, but 0.5 seems like a good default value.

Best features To get some insight in the data, we show the most important SVM features in Table 8. Since the best features were often specific abbreviations, we also show the best features that are also English words.[16] For some DSIs, such as *Cybersecurity*, *E-health* and *E-justice*, the best features make intuitively a lot of sense, and we can be reasonably sure that the model will be able to detect correct documents for this DSI. However, for other DSIs the best features seem overly specific. For example, we do not expect that *beaver* and *lindgren* are good general indicators for *Europeana*, though it does also include more intuitive features, such as *this gallery* and *digital object*. Especially the features for *Online Dispute Resolution* are a bit concerning, since the actual features are mainly abbreviations (that are not that likely to occur in randomly crawled texts), while the word-features do not seem to point to general disputes.

5. Conclusion

One of the goals of the MaCoCu project is improving EU-specific NLP systems that work with Digital Service Infrastructures (DSIs). In this paper, as a necessary and vital first step, we focused on creating a system that can classify texts into specific DSIs. First, we introduced a data set for DSI classification by crawling DSI-specific web domains. We then trained classifiers for English, Spanish and Dutch by fine-tuning a (multilingual) pre-trained language model. The models performed quite well on in-domain data. A manual evaluation of out-of-domain data showed that while DSI-specific data is scarce, we can still find such data with reasonable accuracy. We have already applied our model on two large corpora and made all data, models and predictions publicly available. Future work can then determine whether exploiting such DSI-specific data will indeed lead to improved performance. Finally, we plan to extend our method to more EU (or related) languages, such as Icelandic, Croatian, Bulgarian, Turkish and Slovene.

[16] https://github.com/dwyl/english-words

6. Acknowledgements

The MaCoCu project has received funding from the European Union's Connecting Europe Facility 2014-2020 - CEF Telecom, under Grant Agreement No. INEA/CEF/ICT/A2020/2278341. This communication reflects only the authors' views. The Agency is not responsible for any use that may be made of the information it contains. We thank the Center for Information Technology of the University of Groningen for providing access to the Peregrine high performance computing cluster. Lastly, we thank Mikel L. Forcada for providing us with valuable comments on a draft of this paper.

7. Bibliographical References

Bañón, M., Chen, P., Haddow, B., Heafield, K., Hoang, H., Esplà-Gomis, M., Forcada, M. L., Kamran, A., Kirefu, F., Koehn, P., et al. (2020a). Paracrawl: Web-scale acquisition of parallel corpora. In *Proceedings of the 58th Annual Meeting of the Association for Computational Linguistics*, pages 4555–4567.

Bañón, M., Chen, P., Haddow, B., Heafield, K., Hoang, H., Esplà-Gomis, M., Forcada, M. L., Kamran, A., Kirefu, F., Koehn, P., Ortiz Rojas, S., Pla Sempere, L., Ramírez-Sánchez, G., Sarrías, E., Strelec, M., Thompson, B., Waites, W., Wiggins, D., and Zaragoza, J. (2020b). ParaCrawl: Web-scale acquisition of parallel corpora. In *Proceedings of the 58th Annual Meeting of the Association for Computational Linguistics*, pages 4555–4567, Online, July. Association for Computational Linguistics.

Beltagy, I., Peters, M. E., and Cohan, A. (2020). Longformer: The long-document transformer. *arXiv preprint arXiv:2004.05150*.

Ben-David, E., Rabinovitz, C., and Reichart, R. (2020). PERL: Pivot-based domain adaptation for pre-trained deep contextualized embedding models. *Transactions of the Association for Computational Linguistics*, 8:504–521.

Clark, K., Luong, M.-T., Le, Q. V., and Manning, C. D. (2020). ELECTRA: Pre-training text encoders as discriminators rather than generators. In *ICLR*.

Clark, J. H., Garrette, D., Turc, I., and Wieting, J. (2021). Canine: Pre-training an efficient tokenization-free encoder for language representation. *arXiv preprint arXiv:2103.06874*.

Conneau, A., Khandelwal, K., Goyal, N., Chaudhary, V., Wenzek, G., Guzmán, F., Grave, E., Ott, M., Zettlemoyer, L., and Stoyanov, V. (2020). Unsupervised cross-lingual representation learning at scale. In *Proceedings of the 58th Annual Meeting of the Association for Computational Linguistics*, pages 8440–8451, Online, July. Association for Computational Linguistics.

Devlin, J., Chang, M.-W., Lee, K., and Toutanova, K. (2019). BERT: Pre-training of deep bidirectional transformers for language understanding. In *Proceedings of the 2019 Conference of the North American Chapter of the Association for Computational Linguistics: Human Language Technologies, Volume 1 (Long and Short Papers)*, pages 4171–4186, Minneapolis, Minnesota, June. Association for Computational Linguistics.

Freitag, M. and Al-Onaizan, Y. (2016). Fast domain adaptation for neural machine translation. *arXiv preprint arXiv:1612.06897*.

Guo, C., Pleiss, G., Sun, Y., and Weinberger, K. Q. (2017). On calibration of modern neural networks. In *International Conference on Machine Learning*, pages 1321–1330. PMLR.

He, P., Liu, X., Gao, J., and Chen, W. (2021). DeBERTa: Decoding-enhanced BERT with disentangled attention. In *International Conference on Learning Representations*.

Koehn, P., Hoang, H., Birch, A., Callison-Burch, C., Federico, M., Bertoldi, N., Cowan, B., Shen, W., Moran, C., Zens, R., Dyer, C., Bojar, O., Constantin, A., and Herbst, E. (2007). Moses: Open source toolkit for statistical machine translation. In *ACL Companion Volume Proceedings of the Demo and Poster Sessions*, pages 177–180, Prague, Czech Republic, June.

Kohlschütter, C., Fankhauser, P., and Nejdl, W. (2010). Boilerplate detection using shallow text features. In *Proceedings of the third ACM international conference on Web search and data mining*, pages 441–450.

Lewis, M., Liu, Y., Goyal, N., Ghazvininejad, M., Mohamed, A., Levy, O., Stoyanov, V., and Zettlemoyer, L. (2020). BART: Denoising sequence-to-sequence pre-training for natural language generation, translation, and comprehension. In *Proceedings of the 58th Annual Meeting of the Association for Computational Linguistics*, pages 7871–7880, Online, July. Association for Computational Linguistics.

Li, Z., Wei, Y., Zhang, Y., and Yang, Q. (2018). Hierarchical attention transfer network for cross-domain sentiment classification. In *Proceedings of the AAAI Conference on Artificial Intelligence*, volume 32.

Liu, Y., Ott, M., Goyal, N., Du, J., Joshi, M., Chen, D., Levy, O., Lewis, M., Zettlemoyer, L., and Stoyanov, V. (2019). Roberta: A robustly optimized bert pretraining approach. *arXiv preprint arXiv:1907.11692*.

Lösch, A., Mapelli, V., Piperidis, S., Vasiļjevs, A., Smal, L., Declerck, T., Schnur, E., Choukri, K., and van Genabith, J. (2018). European language resource coordination: Collecting language resources for public sector multilingual information management. In *Proceedings of the Eleventh International Conference on Language Resources and Evaluation (LREC 2018)*, Miyazaki, Japan, May. European Language Resources Association (ELRA).

Luong, M.-T. and Manning, C. (2015). Stanford neural machine translation systems for spoken language domains. In *Proceedings of the 12th International Workshop on Spoken Language Translation: Evaluation Campaign*, pages 76–79, Da Nang, Vietnam, December 3-4.

Pedregosa, F., Varoquaux, G., Gramfort, A., Michel, V., Thirion, B., Grisel, O., Blondel, M., Prettenhofer, P., Weiss, R., Dubourg, V., Vanderplas, J., Passos, A., Cournapeau, D., Brucher, M., Perrot, M., and Duchesnay, E. (2011). Scikit-learn: Machine learning in Python. *Journal of Machine Learning Research*, 12:2825–2830.

Speer, R. (2019). ftfy. Zenodo. Version 5.5.

Wang, R., Utiyama, M., Liu, L., Chen, K., and Sumita, E. (2017). Instance weighting for neural machine translation domain adaptation. In *Proceedings of the 2017 Conference on Empirical Methods in Natural Language Processing*, pages 1482–1488, Copenhagen, Denmark, September. Association for Computational Linguistics.

Wolf, T., Debut, L., Sanh, V., Chaumond, J., Delangue, C., Moi, A., Cistac, P., Rault, T., Louf, R., Funtowicz, M., Davison, J., Shleifer, S., von Platen, P., Ma, C., Jernite, Y., Plu, J., Xu, C., Scao, T. L., Gugger, S., Drame, M., Lhoest, Q., and Rush, A. M. (2020). Transformers: State-of-the-art natural language processing. In *Proceedings of the 2020 Conference on Empirical Methods in Natural Language Processing: System Demonstrations*, pages 38–45, Online, October. Association for Computational Linguistics.

Yang, Z., Dai, Z., Yang, Y., Carbonell, J., Salakhutdinov, R. R., and Le, Q. V. (2019). Xlnet: Generalized autoregressive pretraining for language understanding. *Advances in neural information processing systems*, 32.

A. Bitextor settings

```
# BASIC VARIABLES
dataDir: ~/dsis/e-health/perm/data
permanentDir: ~/dsis/e-health/perm
transientDir: ~/dsis/e-health/trans

until: "split"
profiling: true

# DATA SOURCES - CRAWLING
hostsFile: ~/dsis/e-health.txt
crawler: "wget"
crawlTimeLimit: "96h"

# PREPROCESSING
shards: 8 # 2^8 = 256 shards
batches: 1024 # chunks of 1024 MB

langs: ['en', 'es', 'nl']

preprocessor: "warc2preprocess"
ftfy: true
boilerplateCleaning: true
parser: "simple"
```

Figure 4: Bitextor configuration file.

B. Hyperparameters

Parameter	Range
Learning rate	$10^{-7}, 10^{-6}, 5 \times 10^{-6}, \mathbf{10^{-5}}, 5 \times 10^{-5}$
Batch size	$\{8, \mathbf{12}, 16, 24, 32\}$
Warmup	$\{0.05, \mathbf{0.1}, 0.2, 0.3, 0.5\}$
Label smoothing	$\{0.05, \mathbf{0.1}\}$
Dropout	$\{0.0, 0.05, \mathbf{0.1}, 0.15, 0.2, 0.3\}$
LR decay	$\{\mathbf{0}, 0.01, 0.05, 0.1\}$
Max grad norm	$\{0.5, \mathbf{1}, 1.5, 2\}$

Table 9: Hyperparameter range and final values (bold) for our final English (DEBERTA) and multilingual Spanish/Dutch models (XLM-R). Hyperparameters not included are left at their default value.

C. Web-crawled domains

DSI	Domains
Cybersecurity	www.enisa.europa.eu, ecsc.eu, www.concordia-h2020.eu, www.ccn-cert.cni.es www.incibe-cert.es, maltacip.gov.mt, csirt.cy, csirt.cynet.ac.cy
EESSI	ec.europa.eu
E-health	ehealth-hub.eu, ehtel.eu, digitalhealtheurope.eu
E-justice	e-justice.europa.eu, www.notariesofeurope.eu, www.ejn-crimjust.europa.eu, www.ejnforum.eu www.eurojust.europa.eu, www.ccbe.eu, eubailiff.eu, eur-lex.europa.eu
Europeana	europeana.eu
ODR	accademiadr.it, atlantique-mediation.org, batirmediation-conso.fr, begravningar.se, bekeltetes-csongrad.hu, bekeltetes.hu, conciliazione.a2a.eu conciliazione.gruppoiren.it, conso.immomediateurs.com, ...
Open Data Portal	data.europa.eu, stirdata.eu
Safer-internet	www.betterinternetforkids.eu, www.saferinternetday.org, inhope.org

Table 10: Web-crawled domains. All the domains will be available at the repository provided in Section 3.

D. Detailed scores

	English						Spanish						Dutch					
	Dev			Test			Dev			Test			Dev			Test		
DSI	P	R	F_1	P	R	F_1	P	R	F_1	P	R	F_1	P	R	F_1	P	R	F_1
Cybersecurity	60.5	73.2	66.2	55.3	58.9	57.0	77.3	82.4	79.4	77.8	77.7	77.7	64.6	58.3	61.3	71.5	63.9	67.5
EESSI	64.6	66.9	65.7	66.7	69.9	68.8	79.7	76.8	78.2	79.8	81.6	80.7	45.8	81.8	58.7	43.4	77.8	55.8
E-health	75.0	77.2	76.1	70.4	75.7	72.9	—	—	—	—	—	—	—	—	—	—	—	—
E-justice	70.9	47.7	57.0	69.5	58.6	63.6	68.7	60.7	64.4	69.1	60.4	64.5	85.7	64.0	73.3	84.1	69.5	76.1
Europeana	89.6	78.3	83.6	85.6	59.6	70.3	89.4	82.8	85.9	87.5	81.1	84.2	—	—	—	—	—	—
ODR	75.7	64.6	69.1	71.0	52.7	60.5	74.0	58.3	65.2	71.9	51.9	60.3	37.0	6.4	10.9	70.7	25.3	37.3
Open Data Portal	55.4	50.1	52.6	51.2	45.6	48.3	—	—	—	—	—	—	38.2	68.4	49.1	38.0	62.3	47.2
Safer Internet	74.6	82.4	78.3	77.1	81.3	79.2	—	—	—	—	—	—	—	—	—	—	—	—
Other	89.8	93.5	91.6	86.7	93.2	89.8	92.4	90.0	91.2	89.2	89.8	89.5	79.2	92.1	85.2	84.4	92.0	88.0
Macro	72.9	70.3	71.1	70.5	66.2	67.8	80.3	75.2	77.5	79.2	73.7	76.2	58.4	61.8	56.4	65.3	65.1	62.0

Table 11: Full results per DSI for using the best model for all three languages. Results are on the first run of the system, not averaged over three runs as in Table 5.

Proceedings of the 15th Workshop on Building and Using Comparable Corpora (BUCC 2022) @LREC2022, pages 33–42
Marseille, June 25, 2022
© European Language Resources Association (ELRA), licensed under CC-BY-NC

Multilingual Comparative Analysis of Deep-Learning Dependency Parsing Results Using Parallel Corpora

Diego Alves, Božo Bekavac, Marko Tadić
Faculty of Humanities and Social Sciences, University of Zagreb
Ulica Ivana Lučića 3, 10000, Zagreb
{dfvalio, bbekavac, mtadic}@ffzg.hr

Abstract

This article presents a comparative analysis of dependency parsing results for a set of 16 languages, coming from a large variety of linguistic families and genera, whose parallel corpora were used to train a deep-learning tool. Results are analyzed in comparison to an innovative way of classifying languages concerning the head directionality parameter used to perform a quantitative syntactic typological classification of languages. It has been shown that, despite using parallel corpora, there is a large discrepancy in terms of LAS results. The obtained results show that this heterogeneity is mainly due to differences in the syntactic structure of the selected languages, where Indo-European ones, especially Romance languages, have the best scores. It has been observed that the differences in the size of the representation of each language in the language model used by the deep-learning tool also play a major role in the dependency parsing efficacy. Other factors, such as the number of dependency parsing labels may also have an influence on results with more complex labeling systems such as the Polish language.

Keywords: dependency parsing, typology, multilingualism

1. Introduction

Dependency parsing is an important part of Natural Language Processing (NLP) chains which consist of annotating raw texts from tokenization to dependency relations. This specific task concerns the process to analyze the grammatical structure in a sentence and identify syntactic heads as well as the type of the relationship between them (syntactical analysis) (Jurafsky and Martin, 2009).

Since the 1980s, the NLP field has increasingly relied on statistics, probability, and machine learning methods which require a large amount of linguistic data. Unlike other annotation tasks such as POS tagging, dependency parsing annotation is much more complex and expensive. Furthermore, from 2015 onward, the usage of deep learning techniques has been dominant in this field which has provided a great improvement in overall results even for under-resourced languages (Otter et al., 2018).

The focus of the majority of studies regarding dependency parsing is on new methods to improve overall results using existing data. Methods and algorithms are compared in terms of results, however, usually, there is no comparison or analysis of the obtained results considering the syntactic complexity of languages. This is due to the fact that, in general, systems are trained using different data-sets (in terms of size and content) for different languages. The lack of data for under-resourced languages is the usual explanation for worse results with respect to dependency parsing metrics. It is undeniable that the amount of training data plays a crucial role in the performance of deep learning models, however, it is not clear how models deal with different structures of languages when the same type and amount of linguistic data is provided for different languages.

Therefore, our aim in this paper is to propose a multilingual analysis of dependency parsing results considering the syntactic structure of languages (using head directionality parameter). By using parallel annotated corpora, our idea is to scrutinize parsing results obtained with a deep learning model to check how different language structures influence the performance of the chosen tool. Also, our aim is to correlate it with the syntactical characterization of languages concerning the specific syntactic feature of head and dependent position. As presented by Jurafsky and Martin (Jurafsky and Martin, 2021) this is one of the features that plays a role in the performance of graph-based parsers. The idea is to check the degree of influence in dependency parsing of this specific language characteristic.

The paper is composed as follows: Section 2 presents an overview of the related work to this topic. Section 3 describes the campaign design: language and data-sets selection, dependency parsing annotation, and syntactic typological characterization; Section 4 present the obtained results which are discussed in Section 5. In Section 6 we provide conclusions and possible future directions for research.

2. Related Work

The Universal Dependencies (UD) framework (Nivre et al., 2016) proposes a robust set of rules for annotating parts of speech, morphological features, and syntactic dependencies across different human languages allowing multi-lingual data to be annotated with the same set of tags. If the framework can be used to annotate, in a homogeneous way, different languages, there is a lack of annotated parallel corpora that can be used for more precise multilingual comparison studies.

As mentioned in the previous section, many studies

concerning dependency parsing metrics present multilingual perspectives but results cannot be compared in terms of language structure as training sets come from different sources and present different sizes and genres. An example of it is the article presenting UDify tool (Kondratyuk and Straka, 2019) which is a software conceived for PoS-MSD and dependency parsing tagging integrating Multilingual BERT (mBERT) language model (104 languages) (Pires et al., 2019). It is also the case for mainstream NLP tools such as Stanford Core NLP (Manning et al., 2014), UDPipe (Straka and Straková, 2017), sPacy (Honnibal and Montani, 2017) and NLPCube (Boroș et al., 2018).

In the article "Evaluating Language Tools for Fifteen EU-official Under-resourced Languages" (Alves et al., 2020), the authors have compared tools to check the reproducibility of presented results in the official respective articles. The authors, however, used the same heterogeneous corpora as the developers of the tools to train the models, the focus was on the analysis of the discrepancy between obtained results and claimed ones by the tool creators.

Parallel corpora are most often used in machine translation (MT) tasks. Therefore, many studies considering the quality, availability, and performance of tools using this type of data-set do not consider dependency parsing. It is the case of the studies presented by Heiki-Jaan Kaalep and Kaarel Veskis (Kaalep and Veskis, 2007) and Wolfgang Teubert (Teubert, 1996). When parallel corpora are considered for parsing, the analysis is, most generally, focused on the improvement of overall results, not on language comparison, as in (Kuhn, 2005).

Liu and Xu proposed a quantitative syntactic typological analysis of Romance languages using information from corpora annotated for dependency syntactic relations (Liu and Xu, 2012). They have analyzed the overall distribution of dependency directions which enabled them to correlate with the degree of inflectional variation of a language and to classify them diachronically (compared to Latin) and synchronically. Moreover, in a different article (Alzetta et al., 2020), the authors presented a study whose main objective was to identify cross-linguistic quantitative trends in the distribution of syntactic relations in annotated corpora from distinct languages (4 Indo-European ones) by using an algorithm (LISCA - LInguiStically– driven Selection of Correct Arcs) (Dell'Orletta et al., 2013) capable of detecting patterns of syntactic constructions in large datasets. However, results were not correlated to scores of dependency parsing tools and corpora used were not parallel, thus the content part of texts was not a controlled variable.

Typological information has been used in different ways in many studies intending to improve dependency parsing results. It has been proved that typological comparison of languages is a powerful way of increase overall metrics concerning dependency parsing automatic annotation, especially regarding unannotated languages (which do not have any corpora annotated in terms of syntactic relations) and low-resource ones.

One example is the method proposed by Agić (Agić, 2017) where he combines three language comparison techniques to determine the best single source for an unannotated language: part-of-speech trigrams, a language identification software (lang.py tool, developed by (Litschko et al., 2020)), and WALS features. It considers the whole corpus of the unannotated language to determine the best (most similar in terms of the described comparison features) training corpus. Later, it has been showed by (Litschko et al., 2020) that better results are obtained when typologically analysing each sentence of the unannotated language in comparison with the available annotated corpora, defining, for each instance the best model (and not the same one for the whole text). In both studies, only qualitative typological features and surface level word order (part-of-speech trigrams) are considered.

While the studies mentioned in the previous paragraph focus on part-of-speech trigrams to compare languages, (Wang and Eisner, 2018) proposed a method to compare word order (in terms of part-of-speech possible combinations) by using a deep-learning algorithm (multilayer perceptron architecture) that classify languages in an unsupervised way with the information extracted from delexicalized corpora. This model is, then, used to the identification of the best language to serve as the source of the best training corpus for the target one. Their major aim was to prove that part-of-speech (POS) sequences carry useful information about the syntax of a language.

A different approach, using only typological information from URIEL database (lang2vec tool, (Littell et al., 2017)), was presented by (Glavaš and Vulić, 2021). Their method consists of comparing the vector composed by the values of the linguistic features of the target language with vectors from other well-resourced languages. The idea is not to select the best corpus but to combine the most similar ones from different languages as long as the similarity respects a determined threshold.

These studies have in common the objective of choosing the best combination of languages to improve dependency parsing results, there is no specific analysis concerning the influence of the chosen features used to compare languages on the final results.

In a different perspective, (de Lhoneux et al., 2018) compared how typological features are related to the dependency parsing results when twenty-seven diverse deep-learning parameters are used for cross-lingual parameters sharing. They were divided in three sets: character based one-layer (bidirectional LSTM), word based two-layer (bidirectional LSTM), and multilayered perceptron (MLP) with a single layer. The authors have shown that the linguistic intuition that character- and word-level LSTMs are highly sensitive to phonological and morphosyntactic differences (such as word order), whereas the MLP learns to predict less idiosyncratic, hierarchical relations from relatively abstract representations of parser configurations. Languages were compared in terms of their genealogical family and subject, verb and object order (qualitative classification).

3. Experimental Design

In this section, we describe the corpora that have been used in this study, the dependency parsing task evaluation using UDify software, and the typological classification method that has been employed.

3.1. Languages and Data-set Selection

The data-sets used for all experiments are part of the Parallel Universal Dependencies (PUD) tree-banks created for the CoNLL 2017 shared task on Multilingual Parsing from Raw Text to Universal Dependencies. They are composed of 1000 sentences for each language, always in the same order, coming from the news domain and Wikipedia (Zeman et al., 2017).

The first 750 sentences are originally in English and the rest are in German, French, Italian or Spanish. Sentences were mostly translated by professional translators via the English text. The data has been annotated morphologically and syntactically by Google according to Google universal annotation guidelines, afterwards, labels were converted to Universal Dependencies v2 guidelines[1].

The corpora were composed to serve as test sets to the mentioned shared task. Due to their relatively small size, the creators have suggested that a ten-fold cross-validation should be employed should these sets be used as training ones (as it is the case in this article). As our aim was to focus on one specific syntactic feature, the idea was to use only parallel corpora so that there would be no bias concerning the size or the domain of corpora. No data augmentation technique was used as there is no other parallel annotated corpora covering all PUD languages.

The list of PUD languages, their ISO-639-3 code and their genealogical information according to WALS[2] (Dryer and Haspelmath, 2013) is presented in the table 1. Although WALS database provides valuable information of word order patterns, there is no information regarding the relative position of the head and dependent in a broader way. Their focus is on word order position of subject, object and verb (and other type of syntactic functions), not exactly specifying the behavior of the ensemble of heads and dependents.

All corpora have been tagged in terms of core part-of-speech categories (UPOS) and dependency relation (deprel) using Universal Dependencies labels. The number of UPOS and deprel labels varies depending on the language, their distribution is presented in the tables 2 and 3.

Language	Code	Family	Genus
Arabic	arb	Afro-Asiatic	Semitic
Chinese	cmn	Sino-Tibetan	Chinese
Czech	ces	Indo-European	Slavic
English	eng	Indo-European	Germanic
Finnish	fin	Uralic	Finnic
French	fra	Indo-European	Romance
German	deu	Indo-European	Germanic
Hindi	hin	Indo-European	Indic
Icelandic	isl	Indo-European	Germanic
Indonesian	ind	Austro-nesian	Malayo-Sumbawn
Italian	ita	Indo-European	Romance
Japanese	jpn	Japanese	Japanese
Korean	kor	Korean	Korean
Polish	pol	Indo-European	Slavic
Portuguese	por	Indo-European	Romance
Russian	rus	Indo-European	Slavic
Spanish	spa	Indo-European	Romance
Swedish	swe	Indo-European	Germanic
Thai	tha	Tai-Kadai	Kam-Tai
Turkish	tur	Altaic	Turkic

Table 1: List of languages, the respective ISO-639-3 code and the genealogical information

Languages	Number of UPOS labels
kor	13
cmn, tur	15
arb, ces, fin, hin, jpn, spa, swe	16
eng, fra, deu, ita, pol, por, rus, tha	17
isl, ind	18

Table 2: Distribution of the number of UPOS labels (core part-of-speech) for each language in PUD data-set

The CoNLL-U format also presents a column for

[1] https://github.com/UniversalDependencies/UD_English-PUD

[2] https://wals.info/

Languages	Nb. of deprel types	Nb. of deprel sub-types
arb	34	8
cmn	32	12
ces	31	12
eng	36	12
fin	30	14
fra	31	14
deu	33	12
hin	28	10
isl	31	5
ind	33	14
ita	33	7
jpn	25	0
kor	26	8
pol	28	31
por	33	9
rus	31	8
spa	32	9
swe	33	9
tha	33	10
tur	34	7

Table 3: Distribution of the number of deprel labels for each language in PUD data-set

language-specific part-of-speech tag (XPOS). For this feature, not all languages follow the same labeling system. Arabic, Chinese, English, French, German, Hindi, Italian, Korean, Portuguese, Spanish, Turkish and Thai use the same tags to characterize language specific POS, the other languages in PUD either present different sets of tags, or, as it is the case of Finnish and Indonesian, no information at all is provided concerning this feature.

3.2. Dependency Parsing Annotations

UDify tool (Kondratyuk and Straka, 2019) proposes an architecture aimed for PoS-MSD and dependency parsing tagging integrating Multilingual BERT language model (104 languages). It can be fine-tuned using specific corpora (mono or multilingual) to enhance overall results.
We have selected this tool as it presents the state-of-the-art algorithms concerning the specific task of dependency parsing Annotation.
Training parameters were defined as:

- Number of epochs: 80
- Warmup: 500

Other parameters remained the same as proposed by the authors in their configuration file.
As previously mentioned, the size of the PUD corpora is relatively small (1.000 sentences), therefore, a 10-fold-cross-validation was employed. For each experiment, 600 sentences were used for training, 200 for validation and 200 for testing.
We have considered the LAS (labelled attachment score) value, which is the percentage of words that are assigned both the correct syntactic head and the correct dependency label, as the main dependency parsing metric metric.
Since UDify uses Multilingual BERT, and knowing that languages are not equally represented in this model, it is important to present the data distribution of the selected languages inside it (table 4), as it may have an impact on the final dependency parsing results.

Language	Size Range (GB)
eng	[11.314, 22.627]
deu, fra, spa, rus	[2.828, 5.657]
cmn, ita, jpn, pol, por	[1.414, 2.828]
arb, ces, swe	[0.707, 1.414]
fin, ind, kor, tur	[0.354, 0.707]
tha	[0.177, 0.354]
hin	[0.088, 0.177]
isl	[0.022, 0.044]

Table 4: List of languages we consider in mBERT and its pre-training corpus size (Wu and Dredze, 2020)

It is possible to notice that there is a huge discrepancy regarding the amount of data from different languages used to generate multilingual BERT language model.
As expected, English is the language which has the largest pre-training corpus size, followed by German, French, Spanish and Russian. It is possible to observe that the largest mBERT pre-training corpora come from Indo-European languages, only Chinese and Japanese languages are also quite well represented. Icelandic is the one with the smaller pre-training corpus, therefore, not as well represented in this language model as the other languages from PUD corpora.
Thus, even though we use parallel data to understand the influence of the position of head and dependent feature, by using a system based on mBERT introduce a bias regarding the discrepancy of the training data used in this language model. The importance of this bias will be analysed further in this article. We could have chosen a tool which does not depend on language models to conduct our experiments, however, as these models are part of the state-of-the-art concerning dependency parsing, we decided to keep our initial choice to verify how the chosen syntactic feature influences the results of parsing, if it plays an important role or if it is completely minimized.

3.3. Syntactic Typological Characterisation

To analyse the dependency parsing results obtained from different languages using parallel corpora, we propose a quantitative typological approach concerning syntax, more specifically the head directionality parameter, whether the head precedes the dependent (right-

branching) or is after it (left-branching) in the sentence (Fábregas et al., 2015). The extraction of parameters reflect the directionality observed at the surface level (position of head and dependent observed at the sentence level).
The corpora being parallel, therefore containing the same semantic information, allows us to focus on the syntax differences among the selected languages.
Using a python script, we have extracted for each language the existing patterns concerning the relative position in the sentence of the heads and the dependents, as well as the frequency of occurrence of each pattern. All observed patterns concerning the relative position of head and in PUD corpora have been considered.
All observed patterns extracted from the PUD corpora (2,890 in total) have been included in the language vectors. Our aim is to verify the relevance of this quantitative method to predict LAS results.
An example of extracted pattern is the following:

- ADV_aux_precedes_ADJ - head-final or left-branching - It means that the dependent, which is an adverb (ADV) precedes the head which is an adjective (ADJ) and has the syntactic function of an auxiliary (aux). The dependent can be in any position of the sentence previous to the head, not necessarily right before.

- CCONJ_cc_follows_NOUN - head-initial or right-branching - In this case, the dependent, a coordinating conjunction (CCONJ), comes after the head, which is a noun (NOUN), and has the function of coordination (cc). The dependent can be in any position after the head, not necessarily being right next to it.

Therefore, for each language, we have obtained a vector containing all the existing patterns and their frequency. The distances between languages were calculated using R dist() function (Euclidean) and from the obtained distance matrix, we generated a plot with language clusters using R hclust() function, which uses the complete linkage method for hierarchical clustering by default. This particular clustering method defines the cluster distance between two clusters to be the maximum distance between their individual components.

4. Results

In this section, first, we present the LAS results obtained using UDify trained with the different parallel corpora from PUD data-set. Then, we display the results of the typological analysis (clusters in the format of a dendogram).

4.1. Dependency Parsing Results using UDify

Using UDify with 10-fold cross-validation, we were able to obtain LAS results for all PUD languages. LAS scores and the respective standard deviation values are presented in the table 5.

Language	LAS	Std. Dev.
cmn	72.98	2.08
tur	75.34	2.11
hin	76,12	1.12
isl	77.80	2.56
fin	81.15	1.88
arb	82.37	0.70
kor	84.55	1.33
swe	85.13	1.53
ind	85.51	1.26
pol	86.08	1.59
ces	86.34	1.00
eng	87.39	1.28
deu	88.22	0.85
rus	88.22	0.97
por	88.88	0.85
ita	89.74	0.86
spa	90.23	1.20
jpn	90.75	2.11
fra	90.84	1.36

Table 5: LAS and standard deviation results obtained for each language of PUD data-set using UDify and 10-fold cross-validation. Results are presented from lowest to highest LAS score.

Even though parallel corpora were used to train UDify tool, LAS results vary considerably among PUD languages. The lowest LAS score was obtained for Chinese language (72.98) and the highest for French language (90.82), difference of 15.38 points which is much higher than the calculated standard deviation values.
LAS results are higher than 85 for 11 out of the 16 PUD languages considered in this part of the study, which can be considered as relatively satisfying scores considering the small size of the training corpora.
Analysing Indo-European languages, Romance languages tend to have better LAS scores (higher than 90 for French and Spanish), followed by Germanic and Slavic languages, the exception being Icelandic which has the second lowest LAS value (78.12) among the considered languages.
Indonesian and Korean have scores comparable to other Indo-European languages such as Swedish, Polish and Czech (around 85). Finnish and Arabic have lower scores than Indo-European languages but higher than 80 and, therefore, better than Icelandic and Turkish languages.
When we analyse these LAS results together with the training size of mBERT (mean value of the size range), it is possible to calculate the following correlation coefficients:

- Pearson's correlation = 0.37

- Spearman's correlation: 0.73

Thus, it seems that these two variables are strongly correlated following a non-linear monotonic function (as it is attested by the value obtained for Spearman's coefficient).

4.2. Quantitative Syntactic Language Classification

As explained previously in this article, languages were compared and classified considering quantitative information of the patterns of the position of heads and dependents. The figure 1 presents the clusters of languages generated using R' hclust function.

It is possible to observe in this dendogram the main central cluster corresponding to most of Indo-European languages (except for Hindi). Romance languages are grouped in a sub-cluster of the Indo-European one. We can also notice the proximity of English and Swedish (both Germanic) and Russian and Czech (both Slavic). Icelandic, although being a Germanic language, is closer to Polish language when this specific syntactic feature is analysed. Icelandic is presented in the dendogram grouped with the other Slavic languages. German, also a Germanic language, is grouped closer to the Romance group (specially with Italian and French) and not with the other Germanic languages from PUD corpora.

Close to the Germanic/Slavic cluster, it is possible to notice the group containing Thai, Arabic and Indonesian which have no genealogical relation. The two extremes groups are composed, on the left, by Hindi and Japanese, and, on the left by two sub-clusters: Finnish and Turkish (which is expected as similarities between these languages have been previously observed) and Chinese and Korean.

Beside the classification presented in the figure 1, with the syntactic information extracted for each language, it is also possible to analyse the overall tendency of left-branching or right-branching. The table 6 presents the percentage of cases inside each language corpus where the dependent comes before the head in the sentence (left-branching).

With the results presented in the table 6 and in the Figure 2, it is possible to check whether PUD languages are head-initial or head-final. Arabic, Thai and Indonesian are head-initial languages, Japanese also tends towards being head-initial. Oppositely, Turkish and Korean are distinctly head-final languages. Chinese, Romance and Germanic languages, except Icelandic, have a tendency of being head-final (percentage superior to 55 in the table 6). Slavic languages present different patterns, Polish does not present any tendency, Russian and Czech tend to be head-final because of more relaxed word order in Slavic languages.

The correlation coefficients (Spearman's and Pearson's) were calculated using the percentage of heads preceeding dependents and the delta concerning a balanced distribution of directionality (50/50). The obtained results are lower than 0.1, thus, no correlation can be stated concerning this feature.

Language	%
arb	36.33
tha	39.05
ind	41.91
jpn	45.85
pol	49.21
isl	51.08
rus	54.50
fin	55.85
hin	56.10
ita	57.09
ces	57.13
spa	57.79
por	57.94
fra	58.28
swe	58.75
cmn	60.06
eng	63.77
deu	66.81
tur	69.96
kor	79.86

Table 6: Total percentage of occurrences where the dependent precedes the head (left-branching / head-final) in each selected language corpus

5. Discussion

Comparing the results obtained in our campaign to the scores presented by the developers of UDify (Kondratyuk and Straka, 2019), it is possible to notice that, in general, our LAS values for PUD corpora are higher. It may be due to the fact of using different strategies for using PUD as training set. Also, as expected, LAS scores using PUD are not as high as compared to results from other models trained with larger corpora.

We observed that, as expected, the size of the corpus used to train mBERT has a strong positive correlation with the LAS scores, however, it does not explain the ensemble of the results as English has the biggest training corpus but do not provide the best score concerning UDify.

Analysing Indo-European languages results, it is possible to see that, overall, Romance languages are the ones with the highest LAS values. In terms of multilingual BERT, all of them have large pre-training mBERT corpora. French and Spanish have larger pre-training corpora when compared to Portuguese and Italian and UDify performs better for these two languages. Romance languages are grouped in the figure 1, showing similar distribution of patterns concerning head and dependents position when compared to other PUD languages.

English language, which is the one with the largest pre-training mBERT corpus, does not have the highest LAS

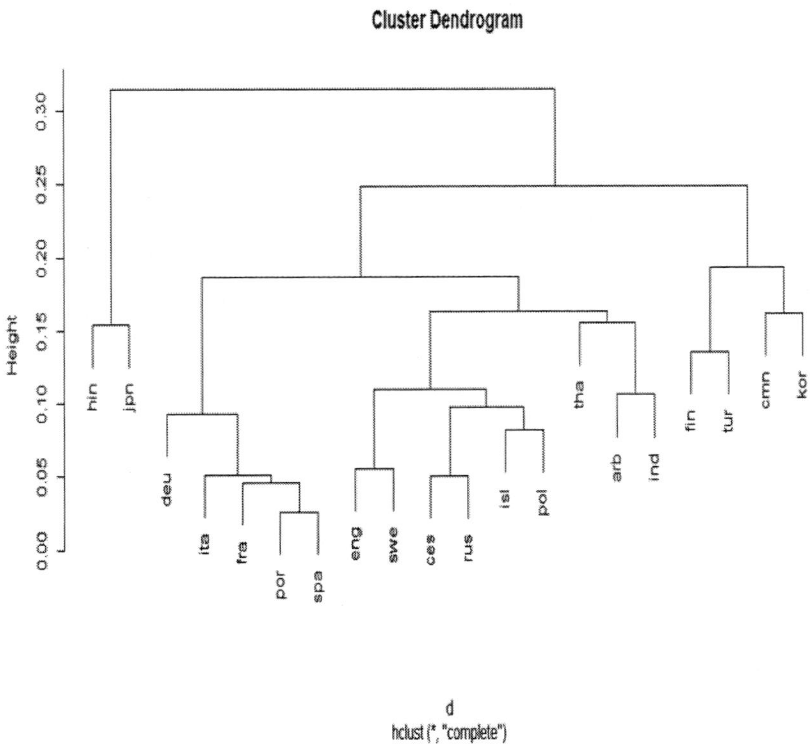

Figure 1: PUD language clusters generated using quantitative analysis of head and dependent position features

score. Its result can be compared to other languages with much smaller mBERT corpus such as Russian, German, Czech and Polish. Thus, it seems that size of the representation of a language in mBERT may play a role only to a certain point when it is used for fine-tuning in parsing tools.

When we observe, more precisely, Germanic and Slavic languages, it is possible to notice that although English and Swedish languages form a sub-cluster, their LAS scores are slightly different. In this case, it may be caused by the discrepancy of the representation of the languages in mBERT. It is the same when we consider Russian and Czech languages.

It is also interesting to observe the sub-cluster formed by Polish and Icelandic inside the group of Indo-European languages. Polish language has a mBERT representation size comparable to Portuguese and Italian, however, its LAS value is much lower. It may be due to its specific syntactic structures as well as to elevated number of deprel labels (59) which is much higher than all the other PUD languages. Icelandic has the second lowest LAS score among PUD languages. Although being a Germanic language, it is not similar in its syntactic structure of heads and dependents when compared to English, Swedish nor German. In addition, Icelandic has the smallest mBERT pre-training corpus which has probably strongly contributed to the low LAS value obtained using UDify.

On the left of the main cluster of Indo-European languages in the Figure 1, we have the sub-cluster formed by Arabic and Indonesian. Both languages have lower LAS scores when compared to Indo-European ones, Indonesian having a better performance even though its mBERT representation is smaller and its number of deprel is higher (47 for Indonesian and 42 for Arabic).

Considering the cluster on the right side of the figure 1, formed by Finnish, Turkish, Chinese and Korean, these languages tend to present lower LAS scores. Finnish, Turkish and Korean have similar size of mBERT representations, but smaller than Indo-European languages. However, their size is comparable to Indonesian which presents better LAS value and, in the figure 1, this language is clustered closer to the Indo-European group. As seen in the table 4, Turkish is a head-final language, it may influence the results. However, Korean language is even more head-final when compared to Turkish and has a better LAS score, however, Korean presents only 34 deprel, while Turkish has 41.

In light of these results, it is possible to notice that differences in the syntactic structures concerning head and dependents may play a role in dependency parsing tools overall results. The size of the language representation

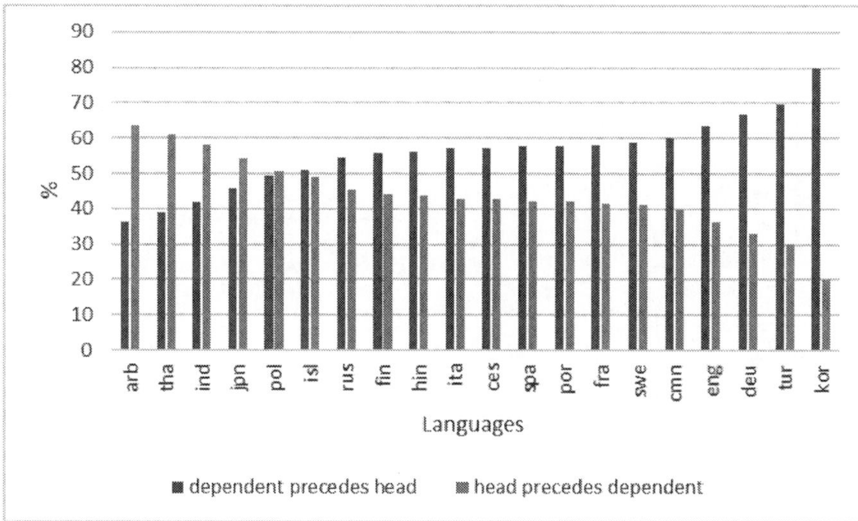

Figure 2: Distribution of the directionality of head and dependent in PUD language corpora

in the language model, however, plays a major role as it helps improving final scores (as it is the case for French and Spanish). Nevertheless, it may not be sufficient to guarantee satisfying LAS result (as it is the case for Turkish).

Also, the parameter of head and dependent position is not the only syntactic feature playing an important role in the observed LAS results, the complexity of the language, represented by the number of deprel labels should be considered as it may have caused the lower LAS value for Polish language (which has a high number of deprel subtypes).

Furthermore, it is important to mention that morphological aspects (whether the language has synthetic or analytical morphology), can also influence the efficacy of the parser. As it can be observed for Finnish and Turkish (both synthetic languages), LAS results are low. However, it is also the case for Chinese, which is an analytical language.

6. Conclusions and Perspectives

In this article we have presented a detailed analysis of dependency parsing results obtained for 16 languages using parallel corpora to understand the differences in the obtained scores considering the specific syntactic feature of head directionality parameter with which we have conducted a quantitative syntactic typological classification.

Thus, we have conducted a series of experiments using UDify tool, using a 10-fold cross-validation to obtain LAS metric for the selected languages. In parallel, we have extracted patterns concerning the position of head and dependents (left or right branching) to generate vectors which were used to compare and classify languages into clusters.

We have observed that, even though parallel corpora were used, different languages present considerably different LAS results. Indo-European languages tend to present better LAS scores, inside this group, Romance languages are the ones that performed the best.

UDify tool uses multilingual mBERT and as the sizes of each language inside this language model are not homogeneous, it was possible to notice that this discrepancy plays a major role in the LAS scores. As expected, languages with larger mBERT representation tend to perform better.

However, the size of the language in mBERT is not the only parameter playing a role in the overall results. English has, by far, the largest size in mBERT and still has a lower LAS score when compared to Romance languages which were all classified the same cluster in our typological study. It is also the case for Russian, which has a mBERT size comparable to French and Spanish for which LAS values are comparable to Portuguese and Italian with smaller mBERT size.

In addition to that, Arabic language has a mBERT representation comparable to Czech and Swedish but its LAS results are not as good as these two languages. Arabic language forms a sub-cluster with Indonesian, not as close to other languages with better performance as it is the case for Czech and Swedish. Also, it is possible to conclude that the size of the language in mBERT and the head and dependent position are not the only aspects influencing the results. Polish language is an example of that, and the reason for the lower LAS value obtained for this language may be the higher number of dependency parsing labels specific of this language.

For future research, it would be interesting to observe how these languages perform in systems which either use more homogeneous language models in terms of language representation or that do not depend on language models at all. Furthermore, specific analysis could be done considering only subject-verb or object-verb directionality.

7. Acknowledgements

The work presented in this paper has received funding from the European Union's Horizon 2020 research and innovation program under the Marie Skłodowska-Curie grant agreement no. 812997 and under the name CLEOPATRA (Cross-lingual Event-centric Open Analytics Research Academy).

8. Bibliographical References

Agić, Ž. (2017). Cross-lingual parser selection for low-resource languages. In *Proceedings of the NoDaLiDa 2017 Workshop on Universal Dependencies (UDW 2017)*, pages 1–10, Gothenburg, Sweden, May. Association for Computational Linguistics.

Alves, D., Thakkar, G., and Tadić, M. (2020). Evaluating language tools for fifteen EU-official under-resourced languages. In *Proceedings of the 12th Language Resources and Evaluation Conference*, pages 1866–1873, Marseille, France, May. European Language Resources Association.

Alzetta, C., Dell'Orletta, F., Montemagni, S., Osenova, P., Simov, K., and Venturi, G. (2020). Quantitative linguistic investigations across universal dependencies treebanks. In Johanna Monti, et al., editors, *Proceedings of the Seventh Italian Conference on Computational Linguistics, CLiC-it 2020, Bologna, Italy, March 1-3, 2021*, volume 2769 of *CEUR Workshop Proceedings*. CEUR-WS.org.

Boroș, T., Dumitrescu, S. D., and Burtica, R. (2018). NLP-cube: End-to-end raw text processing with neural networks. In *Proceedings of the CoNLL 2018 Shared Task: Multilingual Parsing from Raw Text to Universal Dependencies*, pages 171–179, Brussels, Belgium, October. Association for Computational Linguistics.

de Lhoneux, M., Bjerva, J., Augenstein, I., and Søgaard, A. (2018). Parameter sharing between dependency parsers for related languages. In *Proceedings of the 2018 Conference on Empirical Methods in Natural Language Processing*, pages 4992–4997, Brussels, Belgium, October-November. Association for Computational Linguistics.

Dell'Orletta, F., Venturi, G., and Montemagni, S. (2013). Linguistically–driven selection of correct arcs for dependency parsing. *Computación y Sistemas*, 17.

Matthew S. Dryer et al., editors. (2013). *WALS Online*. Max Planck Institute for Evolutionary Anthropology, Leipzig.

Fábregas, A., Mateu, J., and Putnam, M. T. (2015). *Contemporary Linguistic Parameters: Contemporary Studies in Linguistics*. Bloomsbury Academic, London.

Glavaš, G. and Vulić, I. (2021). Climbing the tower of treebanks: Improving low-resource dependency parsing via hierarchical source selection. In *Findings of the Association for Computational Linguistics: ACL-IJCNLP 2021*, pages 4878–4888, Online, August. Association for Computational Linguistics.

Honnibal, M. and Montani, I. (2017). spaCy 2: Natural language understanding with Bloom embeddings, convolutional neural networks and incremental parsing. To appear.

Jurafsky, D. and Martin, J. H. (2009). *Speech and language processing : an introduction to natural language processing, computational linguistics, and speech recognition*. Pearson Prentice Hall, Upper Saddle River, N.J.

Jurafsky, D. and Martin, J. H. (2021). *Speech and Language Processing: An Introduction to Natural Language Processing, Computational Linguistics, and Speech Recognition*. 3rd. (draft) edition.

Kaalep, H.-J. and Veskis, K. (2007). Comparing parallel corpora and evaluating their quality. In *Proceedings of Machine Translation Summit XI: Papers*, Copenhagen, Denmark, September 10-14.

Kondratyuk, D. and Straka, M. (2019). 75 languages, 1 model: Parsing universal dependencies universally.

Kuhn, J. (2005). Parsing word-aligned parallel corpora in a grammar induction context. In Philipp Koehn, et al., editors, *Proceedings of the Workshop on Building and Using Parallel Texts@ACL 2005, Ann Arbor, Michigan, USA, June 29-30, 2005*, pages 17–24. Association for Computational Linguistics.

Litschko, R., Vulić, I., Agić, Ž., and Glavaš, G. (2020). Towards instance-level parser selection for cross-lingual transfer of dependency parsers. In *Proceedings of the 28th International Conference on Computational Linguistics*, pages 3886–3898, Barcelona, Spain (Online), December. International Committee on Computational Linguistics.

Littell, P., Mortensen, D. R., Lin, K., Kairis, K., Turner, C., and Levin, L. (2017). URIEL and lang2vec: Representing languages as typological, geographical, and phylogenetic vectors. In *Proceedings of the 15th Conference of the European Chapter of the Association for Computational Linguistics: Volume 2, Short Papers*, pages 8–14, Valencia, Spain, April. Association for Computational Linguistics.

Liu, H. and Xu, C. (2012). Quantitative typological analysis of romance languages. *Poznań Studies in Contemporary Linguistics*, 48(4):597–625.

Manning, C., Surdeanu, M., Bauer, J., Finkel, J., Bethard, S., and McClosky, D. (2014). The Stanford CoreNLP natural language processing toolkit. In *Proceedings of 52nd Annual Meeting of the Association for Computational Linguistics: System Demonstrations*, pages 55–60, Baltimore, Maryland, June. Association for Computational Linguistics.

Nivre, J., de Marneffe, M.-C., Ginter, F., Goldberg, Y., Hajič, J., Manning, C. D., McDonald, R., Petrov, S.,

Pyysalo, S., Silveira, N., Tsarfaty, R., and Zeman, D. (2016). Universal Dependencies v1: A multilingual treebank collection. In *Proceedings of the Tenth International Conference on Language Resources and Evaluation (LREC'16)*, pages 1659–1666, Portorož, Slovenia, May. European Language Resources Association (ELRA).

Otter, D. W., Medina, J. R., and Kalita, J. K. (2018). A survey of the usages of deep learning in natural language processing. *CoRR*, abs/1807.10854.

Pires, T., Schlinger, E., and Garrette, D. (2019). How multilingual is multilingual BERT? In *Proceedings of the 57th Annual Meeting of the Association for Computational Linguistics*, pages 4996–5001, Florence, Italy, July. Association for Computational Linguistics.

Straka, M. and Straková, J. (2017). Tokenizing, pos tagging, lemmatizing and parsing ud 2.0 with udpipe. In *Proceedings of the CoNLL 2017 Shared Task: Multilingual Parsing from Raw Text to Universal Dependencies*, pages 88–99, Vancouver, Canada, August. Association for Computational Linguistics.

Teubert, W. (1996). Comparable or Parallel Corpora? *International Journal of Lexicography*, 9(3):238–264, 09.

Wang, D. and Eisner, J. (2018). Surface statistics of an unknown language indicate how to parse it. *Transactions of the Association for Computational Linguistics*, 6:667–685.

Wu, S. and Dredze, M. (2020). Are all languages created equal in multilingual bert?

Zeman, D., Popel, M., Straka, M., Hajič, J., Nivre, J., Ginter, F., Luotolahti, J., Pyysalo, S., Petrov, S., Potthast, M., Tyers, F., Badmaeva, E., Gokirmak, M., Nedoluzhko, A., Cinková, S., Hajič jr., J., Hlaváčová, J., Kettnerová, V., Urešová, Z., Kanerva, J., Ojala, S., Missilä, A., Manning, C. D., Schuster, S., Reddy, S., Taji, D., Habash, N., Leung, H., de Marneffe, M.-C., Sanguinetti, M., Simi, M., Kanayama, H., de Paiva, V., Droganova, K., Martínez Alonso, H., Çöltekin, Ç., Sulubacak, U., Uszkoreit, H., Macketanz, V., Burchardt, A., Harris, K., Marheinecke, K., Rehm, G., Kayadelen, T., Attia, M., Elkahky, A., Yu, Z., Pitler, E., Lertpradit, S., Mandl, M., Kirchner, J., Alcalde, H. F., Strnadová, J., Banerjee, E., Manurung, R., Stella, A., Shimada, A., Kwak, S., Mendonça, G., Lando, T., Nitisaroj, R., and Li, J. (2017). CoNLL 2017 shared task: Multilingual parsing from raw text to Universal Dependencies. In *Proceedings of the CoNLL 2017 Shared Task: Multilingual Parsing from Raw Text to Universal Dependencies*, pages 1–19, Vancouver, Canada, August. Association for Computational Linguistics.

Proceedings of the 15th Workshop on Building and Using Comparable Corpora (BUCC 2022) @LREC2022 , pages 43–49
Marseille, June 25, 2022
© European Language Resources Association (ELRA), licensed under CC-BY-NC

CUNI Submission to the BUCC 2022 Shared Task on Bilingual Term Alignment

Borek Požár, Klára Tauchmanová, Kristýna Neumannová,
Ivana Kvapilíková and Ondřej Bojar
Institute of Formal and Applied Linguistics,
Faculty of Mathematics and Physics, Charles University,
Prague, Czech Republic,
pozar.borek@gmail.com, klara.tauchmanova@gmail.com, kristynaneumannova@gmail.com,
kvapilikova@ufal.mff.cuni.cz, bojar@ufal.mff.cuni.cz

Abstract

We present our submission to the BUCC Shared Task on bilingual term alignment in comparable specialized corpora. We devised three approaches using static embeddings with post-hoc alignment, the Monoses pipeline for unsupervised phrase-based machine translation, and contextualized multilingual embeddings. We show that contextualized embeddings from pretrained multilingual models lead to similar results as static embeddings but further improvement can be achieved by task-specific fine-tuning. Retrieving term pairs from the running phrase tables of the Monoses systems can match this enhanced performance and leads to an average precision of 0.88 on the train set.

Keywords: word embeddings, usupervised learning, alignment, multiword expressions, embedding mapping

1. Introduction

The goal of the task is to find equivalent expressions (both one- and multi-word, we will call them *terms*) in two languages. The inputs are comparable corpora C_1 and C_2 in languages L_1, L_2 and lists of terms D_1, D_2 which are to be mapped onto each other, where D_1 is extracted from C_1 and D_2 from C_2. The output $O_{1,2}$ is supposed to be a list of term pairs t_1, t_2 that are translations of each other, where $t_i \in D_i \in L_i$. The output list should be ordered based on decreasing confidence in the translation. Some terms from D_1 may not have a translation in D_2, some may have multiple translations, and conversely. The submission length is limited to $10 \cdot \frac{D_1+D_2}{2}$. For the training, the gold output $G_{1,2}$ is available. Average Precision is used as a metric and the usage of any additional data (except the CCAligned corpus (El-Kishky et al., 2020), from which the datasets were extracted) is allowed.

The training language pair was English-French, the test datasets were supposed to contain three language pairs – English-French, English-German and English-Russian, however only the English-French was released.

We took three different approaches to find the candidate translation pairs. In the first approach, we create static FastText term embeddings, align them and then search for the nearest neighbours in the embedding space (section 3). The second approach uses an unsupervised phrase-based machine translation (MT) system Monoses and searches in its translation tables (section 4). We also experiment with their combination (section 5). The third approach is similar to the first one, but the embeddings are extracted from pretrained multilingual language models (section 6).

2. Related Work

The task of bilingual term alignment is close to the task of bilingual lexicon induction (BLI) which was initially tackled by statistical deciphering (Ravi and Knight, 2011). Later works on BLI are mostly embedding-based, where authors generate two monolingual embedding spaces and align them post-hoc either with the supervision of an existing lexicon (Mikolov et al., 2013) or with a very weak supervision of identical strings and numerals (Artetxe et al., 2017) or no supervision at all (Conneau et al., 2018; Artetxe et al., 2018a). The cross-lingual embedding space is then searched for the nearest neighbours.

Alternatively, Artetxe et al. (2019a) use cross-lingual embeddings to build a phrase-table of an unsupervised statistical MT system which is used to generate a synthetic parallel corpus. The bilingual lexicon is extracted from the synthetic corpus by using statistical word alignment techniques. Shi et al. (2021) combine unsupervised bitext mining and unsupervised word alignment to obtain a lexicon of state-of-the-art quality.

3. First Approach

3.1. Data Preprocessing

Since the first approach is based on the embedding mapping, we needed to merge the multiword expressions to obtain their embeddings. We replaced the spaces in such expressions by underscores, so when splitting on whitespaces, they were treated as one word. In order to replace the right spaces, we needed to find the multiword expressions in the corpus. Since many of the words were in an inflected form, we used lemmatization. We tried UDPipe 1 (Straka and Straková, 2017)

and UDPipe 2 (Straka, 2018), both trained on Universal Dependencies data. The former one was faster (several hours on 1 CPU thread) than the latter one (several hours on GTX1080 GPU), but produced worse results, as expected. All the characters in the corpora were changed to lowercase and numbers were normalized into a <num> token, since their meaning is not important for the task and normalization helps the embeddings training.
Some sentences contained more than one of the term from the list and some of the terms were overlapping, for example the English term list contained terms valid email, email address and valid email address. In order to deal with this, we added all possible versions of the sentence to the corpus, including the original one. That way, the embeddings could be trained for all the terms, which we consider correct, because they all appeared in the sentence. An example original sentence from the corpus please enter a valid email address with an example term list valid email, email address, valid email address would then appear in our training data in four variants:

- please enter a valid_email address
- please enter a valid_email_address
- please enter a valid email_address
- please enter a valid email address

We also needed to lemmatize the term lists. We tried passing the term lists right into the lemmatizer, but that produced very bad results, presumably because the lemmatizers work with a sentence context. Therefore, for each term, we looked at how it was lemmatized in the corpus and used the most frequent lemma. Then after retrieving the translations at the end of this approach, we have converted the lemmatized terms back to their original versions in order to produce the correct output.

3.2. Cross-lingual Word Embeddings

We used an unsupervised method provided by FastText (Bojanowski et al., 2017) to train word vectors for both preprocessed monolingual corpora. Monolingual embeddings of dimension 300 were learned using the skip-gram model with subwords formed from 3 to 6 substring characters.
The obtained monolingual word embeddings were then aligned into a common space using an unsupervised method provided by the MUSE tool (Conneau et al., 2018). The unsupervised method leverages adversarial training to learn a linear mapping from the source to the target space. The training was run for 5 epochs with 1,000,000 iterations per epoch.

3.3. Resulting Term Dictionary

The resulting dictionary was created by computing neighbours of individual terms from the given list of terms. For each term from the source language, we compute k nearest neighbours (for $k = 1, 2, 3, 5, 10$) in the target language. Similarly, we computed k nearest neighbours for each term from the target language. For each translation, we considered the spatial similarity as a score, summing it if we found given translation pair when searching both directions. Then we filter out pairs that contain terms not included in the given list of terms (both from the source and the target language).
Finally, we arranged pairs of terms into the resulting dictionary in the following order: first the nearest neighbour for each source term in an alphabetical order, then the second nearest neighbour, etc. If a source term no longer had another neighbour, it was skipped. Table 1 contains first 30 translations from the train set. The results of this approach are presented in Table 4.

abreast	affût
absence	absence
absolute	absolue
absolute freedom	liberté absolue
absolutely	absolument
academic	académique
acceptable	acceptable
access control	système de contrôle
accessible	accessible
accident	accident
account	compte
account number	numéro de compte
accurate	précises
acid	acide
acoustic	acoustique
action	action
active	actifs
active life	vie active
actively	activement
active members	membres actifs
activists	activistes
activities	activités
actors	actrice
adaptation	adaptation
additional	supplémentaires
additional charge	charge supplémentaire
additional cost	coût supplémentaire
additional income	revenu supplémentaire
additional info	informations supplémentaires
additional information	informations supplémentaires

Table 1: First 30 translations on train set from the first approach.

4. Second Approach

The second approach is based on unsupervised phrase-based machine translation. The model was trained using only the given comparable corpora. As the main component of the pipeline, we used the Monoses tool (Artetxe et al., 2019b). The tool processed raw corpora that were given by the shared task organizers, no other preprocessing was used.

4.1. Monoses Pipeline

The training pipeline of Monoses consists of ten steps and produces a model for translation. For our purpose, we worked with the first eight steps of the pipeline and then extracted the needed information from the resulting phrase tables. The phrase-based translation models during the training are built with Moses (Koehn et al., 2007).

Firstly, Monoses preprocessed both corpora (for target and source language) – each corpus was tokenized, cleaned, truecased and split into training and development parts. In the second step, language models for both languages were trained. After that, phrase embeddings for extracted n-grams were trained with the help of the external tool Phrase2Vec (Artetxe et al., 2018c). The fourth step of the pipeline provided mapping of embeddings of phrases to cross-lingual space with the help of an external tool VecMap (Artetxe et al., 2018b). After that, the initial phrase table was induced for both directions (src to trg and trg to src). Next step built initial translation model for both directions. The seventh step is unsupervised tuning. This step was done using adapted MERT (Artetxe et al., 2019b). To run this step properly, the length initialization had to be chosen. That is because of different length of the input corpora. The last step we performed was the iterative refinement using back-translation. After the translation, the corpora were cleaned, and then aligned using FastAlign (Dyer et al., 2013). A Moses translation model was built from this aligned corpus and new phrase tables were produced. We used this step without tuning and we proceeded only one iteration of back-translation, because the corpora given for this task were too big.

As we discovered, the unsupervised tuning decreased the performance of the model for this particular task (see Table 5). Therefore, in our pipeline, we skipped the step number seven and used the model from the sixth step for further training. We also tried to run the pipeline on lemmatized corpora (preprocessed by Udpipe2 – see Section 3.1), but that decreased the performance as well (see Table 6).

4.2. Processing of Phrase Table

The phrase table created in the eighth step for translation from target to source was used to produce the results. Although the phrase table included all retrieved n-grams, we only considered the rows containing phrases from given lists of terms.

Each line of the phrase table contains a source phrase (in English for this task), a target phrase (in French) and several scores – inverse phrase translation probability, inverse lexical weighting, direct phrase translation probability, direct lexical weighting.

We needed only one score to sort the results according to their reliability, so we multiplied the direct and the inverse translation probability and used the product as the final score for the task. The result was then sorted according to this score and was submitted to the shared task (see example of results on train set: Table 2).

todo	todo	selection	sélection
desc	desc	slightly	légèrement
predecessor	prédécesseur	grade	grade
dramatic	dramatique	conversation	conversation
chapter	chapitre	tribe	tribu
literally	littéralement	mirror	miroir
iframe	iframe	choice	choix
fiction	fiction	formula	formule
propaganda	propagande	gang	gang
succession	succession	region	région
composition	composition	combination	combinaison
ritual	rituel	discussion	discussion
definition	définition	pilot	pilote
group	groupe	comparison	comparaison
compilation	compilation	coverage	couverture
survival	survie	source	source
birth	naissance	preparation	préparation
trackback	trackback	quiz	quiz
stats	stats	passage	passage
partnership	partenariat	resolution	résolution

Table 2: Top 40 translations on train set from second approach.

5. Combination of the Approaches

The main problem with the first approach is that it is not able to compare pairs with a different source term. We tried to overcome this problem by combining the results from the first and the second approach. Namely, we took pairs of terms acquired from the first approach and we arranged them in the following order: first the source terms with their nearest neighbour sorted by the scores obtained from the second approach, then the source terms with the second nearest neighbour again sorted by the scores from the second approach, etc. Table 3 contains top 40 translation for the train set. The results of this approach are summarized in Table 6.

6. Third Approach

Similar to the first approach, this method uses term embeddings to match corresponding term pairs based on their adjusted cosine similarity. It differs in the way we obtain the bilingual word embeddings and in the metric we use in the nearest neighbour search.

6.1. Corpus Preprocessing

We first matched the term occurrences in the training corpora and joined individual words composing a term with an underscore (e.g. phone_number, email_address). We then tokenized the corpora using

desc	desc	navigation	navigation
birth	naissance	group	groupe
tribe	tribu	formula	formule
composition	composition	population	population
difference	différence	conversation	conversation
generation	génération	region	région
combination	combinaison	existence	existence
neutral	neutre	gang	gang
choice	choix	selection	sélection
anti	anti	preparation	préparation
inhabitants	habitants	officially	officiellement
definition	définition	traditionally	traditionnellement
presence	présence	role	rôle
points	points	protection	protection
planet	planète	automatically	automatiquement
stock	stock	minutes	minutes
directly	directement	massage	massage
possession	possession	resolution	résolution
distinction	distinction	easily	facilement
residence	résidence	creation	création

Table 3: Top 40 translations on train set from combination of the approaches.

the Hugging Face pretrained tokenizers[1] to modify the input into the form each model expects it.

6.2. Multilingual Language Models

In contrast to the static embeddings used in the first approach, we experimented with contextualized embeddings from multilingual BERT (Devlin et al., 2018) and XLM (Conneau and Lample, 2019) model. The models we used have 12 and 16 layers, respectively, each of which encodes every subword into a vector of 756 and 1280 elements, respectively. We followed the method of Kvapilikova et al. (2020) to bring the XLM embeddings closer together by fine-tuning the model on a small portion of parallel sentences using the TLM objective (Conneau and Lample, 2019). According to the previous research, the parallel sentences used for fine-tuning do not have to match the language pair of interest so we experimented with English-German sentences from the News Commentary as well as English-French data provided for this task. The English-French parallel sentences were mined from the monolingual training data using the LASER sentence embeddings (Artetxe and Schwenk, 2019) where we retrieved the first 300,000 matching pairs. We also experimented with monolingual fine-tuning on the training corpora using the masked language model (MLM) (Devlin et al., 2018) objective.

The fine-tuning was performed in the XLM toolkit (`https://github.com/facebookresearch/XLM`) provided by the authors of the model with the Adam (Kingma and Ba, 2015) optimizer and the learning rate of 0.00005.

[1] `https://huggingface.co/docs/transformers/main_classes/tokenizer`

6.3. Term Embeddings

We took the embeddings from the 5th-to-last layer of the models as the mid-layers of the models carry the most multilingual information (Kvapilikova et al., 2020; Pires et al., 2019). Each word is composed of subwords and some terms have more than one word. We calculated the contextualized term embedding by averaging the embeddings of the subwords it contains. The embeddings are context-dependent. In order to get rid of this dependence, we took an average of the contextualized embeddings for one term over all the contexts from the training data set. This method is also referred to as the average anchor method (Schuster et al., 2019).

6.4. Term Retrieval

We used cosine similarity with Cross-modal Local Scaling (CSLS) (Conneau et al., 2018) to retrieve the term translation candidates. To compile the term dictionary, we keep only the closest candidate for each source term and sort the term pairs by their CSLC scores. The results are summarized in Table 7.

7. Evaluation

The evaluation of the task was done with the Mean Average Precision (MAP) metric. Our models produced a bilingual term pair list. The relevance of a term pair was determined by its presence in the gold dictionary ($D_{1,2}$).

Precision for *k* (see Formula 1) was computed as *k* divided by the size of the set of predicted term pairs from the top to the position where *k* relevant term pairs were retrieved (R_k).

Mean Average Precision (MAP) is then the sum over all *k* to the size of the golden dictionary (*m*) of precisions for *k* divided by *m* (see Formula 2).

$$P(R_k) = \frac{|R_k \cap D_{1,2}|}{|R_k|} \quad (1)$$

$$MAP = \frac{1}{m} \sum_{k=1}^{m} P(R_k) \quad (2)$$

7.1. Train Results

We present results for our three approaches on the train set (English-French language pair). The Table 4 presents results of the first approach. Results are divided according to the preprocessing used (UDPipe 1 or UDPipe 2) and to the number of computed nearest neighbours (for $k = 1, 2, 3, 5, 10$). The table shows the size of the terms dictionary, number of correct terms and Mean Average Precision. The best results were obtained for UDPipe 2 preprocessing and $k = 2$.

Overall we can conclude that this method is very precise when retrieving the nearest neighbour only. Including more neighbours increases the resulting dictionary size dramatically with only negligible effect on MAP. This effect is not that strong when using UDPipe

2 for preprocessing, presumably because it is more accurate and many of the second neighbours are translations already found in the other direction. As we have already mentioned, our theory is that the MAP does not raise significantly mainly, because we are unable to rank the translations correctly. Quite probably there are a lot of terms which have only 1 correct translation, however when using more neighbours, we include more translations for each of the terms, lowering the precision dramatically while raising the recall only marginally.

Method		Size	Correct terms	MAP
UDPipe 1	1nn	2504	2083	0.717
	2nn	4080	2178	**0.723**
	3nn	4452	2182	0.720
	5nn	6217	2218	0.712
	10nn	10113	2265	0.695
UDPipe 2	1nn	2225	1981	0.700
	2nn	3419	2131	**0.728**
	3nn	4459	2181	0.724
	5nn	6356	2237	0.713
	10nn	10398	2287	0.693
Gold dictionary		2519	2519	

Table 4: Approach 1 results on train set.

The scores for the second approach based on the phrased-based translation system are generally higher than for the first approach (see Table 5), but for the price of a bigger resulting dictionary. The best results were produced when skipping the tuning step and with no lemmatization during preprocessing.

Method	Size	MAP
Monoses – with tuning	6596	0.86
Monoses – no tuning	17087	**0.88**
Monoses – lemmatized, no tuning	31506	0.78
Gold dictionary	2519	

Table 5: Approach 2 results on train set.

As we can see from the results, this approach gets higher MAP score, however the sizes of the dictionaries are much bigger, so the model is not very precise. We assume it benefits strongly from the ability to rank produced translation pairs correctly, which allows it to get such a high MAP even with dictionaries that are big. It may be interesting to take only some of the highest scoring translations, we did not look into this though.

The results from the combination of the first two approaches are listed in the Table 6. When using UDPipe 1 for preprocessing, the best scores is obtained for $k = 1$. On the other hand, the best scores for UDPipe 2 preprocessing is acquired for $k = 10$. The overall best score is reached for $k = 10$ and UDPipe 2 for preprocessing, ordering the candidates according to the winning Monoses results.

Method			Size	MAP
Monoses with tuning	UDPipe 1	1nn	2504	**0.769**
		3nn	4452	0.762
		5nn	6217	0.760
		10nn	10113	0.750
	UDPipe 2	1nn	2225	0.766
		3nn	4459	0.833
		5nn	6356	0.838
		10nn	10398	**0.857**
Monoses without tuning	UDPipe 1	1nn	2504	**0.770**
		3nn	4452	0.761
		5nn	6217	0.759
		10nn	10113	0.750
	UDPipe 2	1nn	2225	0.772
		3nn	4459	0.842
		5nn	6356	0.857
		10nn	10398	**0.867**
Lemmatized monoses without tuning	UDPipe 1	1nn	2504	**0.764**
		3nn	4452	0.757
		5nn	6217	0.754
		10nn	10113	0.744
	UDPipe 2	1nn	2225	0.762
		3nn	4459	0.828
		5nn	6356	0.843
		10nn	10398	**0.851**

Table 6: Approach combination results on train set.

	Model	MAP
1	FastText + MUSE	0.859
2	bert-base-cased	0.783
3	xlm-mlm-100-1280	0.837
4	(3) + fine-tune MLM (en,fr)	0.871
5	(4) + fine-tune TLM (en-fr)	**0.897**
6	(3) + fine-tune TLM (en-fr)	0.880
7	(3) + fine-tune TLM (en-de)	0.881

Table 7: Approach 3 results on train set.

With this combination we have tried to leverage advantages of the two approaches – getting a better precision as the approach 1 and a better ranking as the approach 2. It mostly fulfilled our expectations, the best approach has only around 1 % lower MAP with a dictionary almost half the size.

We decided to submit three test runs according to these results, namely the term dictionaries from the first approach using UDPipe 2 preprocessing and $k = 2$, the second approach applied to raw corpora without tuning and their combination with $k = 10$.

The third approach was not finalized in time to be submitted to the official BUCC 2022 shared task on English-French term translation but we nevertheless include the results on the train set for completeness and comparison. Given the favorable results, we planned to use this approach for the German and Russian test sets, possibly in a future round of this task.

All scores in Table 7 were obtained using the CSLS metric for nearest neighbour search and dictionary creation. We compare contextualized multilingual embeddings from the 5th-to-last layer of the pretrained models with a baseline of static bilingual embeddings with 100 elements trained by FastText and aligned using MUSE with no supervision and see that the pretrained models do not reach the baseline but the XLM-100 model performs significantly better than the BERT-base model. Fine-tuning the XLM-100 model on the task-specific texts provided for training brings the results over the baseline, especially when using the quasi-parallel sentences retrieved by LASER. Interestingly, in agreement with the findings of (Kvapilikova et al., 2020), fine-tuning on completely unrelated parallel sentences (English-German) leads to an almost identical improvement.

8. Conclusion

We designed three approaches to bilingual term alignment. We searched for the nearest neighbours in the term embedding space created by a static FastText embedding model with post-hoc alignment (Approach 1) and pretrained multilingual language models (Approach 3). We also used an unsupervised phrase-based machine translation system created from the training data and searched its phrase tables for term pair candidates (Approach 2). The latter approach leads to similar results on the train set but only the Approach 1 and Approach 2 were finished in time to be submitted for the test run.

We learned that the pretrained multilingual model XLM-100 and its universal contextualized embeddings lead to a similar performance as static embeddings trained on the task-specific training corpus. However, the static embeddings have a significantly lower embedding size (300 in contrast to 1280 of the XLM-100 model) so the comparison is not straightforward. When fine-tuning the XLM model with task-specific data, we were able to push the precision higher from 0.837 to 0.897 (MAP on train set).

9. Acknowledgements

This work has received funding from the grant 19-26934X (NEUREM3) of the Czech Science Foundation, and support from the project "Grant Schemes at CU" (reg. no. CZ.02.2.69/0.0/0.0/19_073/0016935). This research was partially supported by SVV project number 260 575.

10. Bibliographical References

Artetxe, M. and Schwenk, H. (2019). Massively multilingual sentence embeddings for zero-shot cross-lingual transfer and beyond. *Transactions of the Association for Computational Linguistics*, 7:597–610.

Artetxe, M., Labaka, G., and Agirre, E. (2017). Learning bilingual word embeddings with (almost) no bilingual data. In *Proceedings of the 55th Annual Meeting of the Association for Computational Linguistics (Volume 1: Long Papers)*, pages 451–462, Vancouver, Canada, July. Association for Computational Linguistics.

Artetxe, M., Labaka, G., and Agirre, E. (2018a). A robust self-learning method for fully unsupervised cross-lingual mappings of word embeddings. In *Proceedings of the 56th Annual Meeting of the Association for Computational Linguistics (Volume 1: Long Papers)*, pages 789–798, Melbourne, Australia, July. Association for Computational Linguistics.

Artetxe, M., Labaka, G., and Agirre, E. (2018b). A robust self-learning method for fully unsupervised cross-lingual mappings of word embeddings. In *Proceedings of the 56th Annual Meeting of the Association for Computational Linguistics (Volume 1: Long Papers)*, pages 789–798.

Artetxe, M., Labaka, G., and Agirre, E. (2018c). Unsupervised statistical machine translation. In *Proceedings of the 2018 Conference on Empirical Methods in Natural Language Processing*, pages 3632–3642, Brussels, Belgium, November. Association for Computational Linguistics.

Artetxe, M., Labaka, G., and Agirre, E. (2019a). Bilingual lexicon induction through unsupervised machine translation. In *Proceedings of the 57th Annual Meeting of the Association for Computational Linguistics*, pages 5002–5007, Florence, Italy, July. Association for Computational Linguistics.

Artetxe, M., Labaka, G., and Agirre, E. (2019b). An effective approach to unsupervised machine translation. In *Proceedings of the 57th Annual Meeting of the Association for Computational Linguistics*, pages 194–203, Florence, Italy, July. Association for Computational Linguistics.

Bojanowski, P., Grave, E., Joulin, A., and Mikolov, T. (2017). Enriching word vectors with subword information. *Transactions of the Association for Computational Linguistics*, 5:135–146.

Conneau, A. and Lample, G. (2019). Cross-lingual language model pretraining. In H. Wallach, et al., editors, *Advances in Neural Information Processing Systems 32*, pages 7059–7069. Curran Associates, Inc.

Conneau, A., Lample, G., Ranzato, M., Denoyer, L., and Jégou, H. (2018). Word translation without parallel data. In *6th International Conference on Learning Representations (ICLR 2018)*.

Devlin, J., Chang, M., Lee, K., and Toutanova, K. (2018). BERT: pre-training of deep bidirectional transformers for language understanding. *arXiv [e-Print archive]*, abs/1810.04805.

Dyer, C., Chahuneau, V., and Smith, N. A. (2013). A simple, fast, and effective reparameterization of IBM model 2. In *Proceedings of the 2013 Conference of the North American Chapter of the Association for Computational Linguistics: Human Language Tech-*

nologies, pages 644–648, Atlanta, Georgia, June. Association for Computational Linguistics.

El-Kishky, A., Chaudhary, V., Guzmán, F., and Koehn, P. (2020). CCAligned: A massive collection of cross-lingual web-document pairs. In *Proceedings of the 2020 Conference on Empirical Methods in Natural Language Processing (EMNLP 2020)*, pages 5960–5969, Online, November. Association for Computational Linguistics.

Kingma, D. P. and Ba, J. (2015). Adam: A method for stochastic optimization. In *Proceedings of the 3rd International Conference for Learning Representations*.

Koehn, P., Hoang, H., Birch, A., Callison-Burch, C., Federico, M., Bertoldi, N., Cowan, B., Shen, W., Moran, C., Zens, R., Dyer, C., Bojar, O., Constantin, A., and Herbst, E. (2007). Moses: Open source toolkit for statistical machine translation. In *Proceedings of the 45th Annual Meeting of the Association for Computational Linguistics Companion Volume Proceedings of the Demo and Poster Sessions*, pages 177–180, Prague, Czech Republic, June. Association for Computational Linguistics.

Kvapilikova, I., Artetxe, M., Labaka, G., Agirre, E., and Bojar, O. (2020). Unsupervised multilingual sentence embeddings for parallel corpus mining. In *Proceedings of the 58th Annual Meeting of the Association for Computational Linguistics: Student Research Workshop*. In print.

Mikolov, T., Le, Q. V., and Sutskever, I. (2013). Exploiting similarities among languages for machine translation. *CoRR*, abs/1309.4168.

Pires, T., Schlinger, E., and Garrette, D. (2019). How multilingual is multilingual BERT? In *Proceedings of the 57th Annual Meeting of the Association for Computational Linguistics*, pages 4996–5001, Florence, Italy, July. Association for Computational Linguistics.

Ravi, S. and Knight, K. (2011). Deciphering foreign language. In *Proceedings of the 49th Annual Meeting of the Association for Computational Linguistics: Human Language Technologies*, pages 12–21, Portland, Oregon, USA, June. Association for Computational Linguistics.

Schuster, T., Ram, O., Barzilay, R., and Globerson, A. (2019). Cross-lingual alignment of contextual word embeddings, with applications to zero-shot dependency parsing. In *Proceedings of the 2019 Conference of the North American Chapter of the Association for Computational Linguistics: Human Language Technologies, Volume 1 (Long and Short Papers)*, pages 1599–1613, Minneapolis, Minnesota, June. Association for Computational Linguistics.

Shi, H., Zettlemoyer, L., and Wang, S. I. (2021). Bilingual lexicon induction via unsupervised bitext construction and word alignment. In *Proceedings of the 59th Annual Meeting of the Association for Computational Linguistics and the 11th International Joint Conference on Natural Language Processing (Volume 1: Long Papers)*, pages 813–826, Online, August. Association for Computational Linguistics.

Straka, M. and Straková, J. (2017). Tokenizing, pos tagging, lemmatizing and parsing ud 2.0 with udpipe. In *Proceedings of the CoNLL 2017 Shared Task: Multilingual Parsing from Raw Text to Universal Dependencies*, pages 88–99, Vancouver, Canada, August. Association for Computational Linguistics.

Straka, M. (2018). UDPipe 2.0 prototype at CoNLL 2018 UD shared task. In *Proceedings of the CoNLL 2018 Shared Task: Multilingual Parsing from Raw Text to Universal Dependencies*, pages 197–207, Brussels, Belgium, October. Association for Computational Linguistics.

Proceedings of the 15th Workshop on Building and Using Comparable Corpora (BUCC 2022) @LREC2022 , pages 50–55
Marseille, June 25, 2022
© European Language Resources Association (ELRA), licensed under CC-BY-NC

Challenges of Building Domain-Specific Parallel Corpora from Public Administration Documents

Filip Klubička[1,2], Lorena Kasunić[1], Danijel Blazsetin[1], Petra Bago[1]
[1]University of Zagreb, Faculty of Humanities and Social Sciences, Zagreb, Croatia
Ivana Lučića 3, 10 000 Zagreb, Croatia
[2]Technological University Dublin, ADAPT Centre, Dublin, Ireland
filip.klubicka@adaptcentre.ie, {lorena.kasunic, blazsetin7}@gmail.com, pbago@ffzg.hr

Abstract

PRINCIPLE was a Connecting Europe Facility (CEF)-funded project that focused on the identification, collection and processing of language resources (LRs) for four European under-resourced languages (Croatian, Icelandic, Irish and Norwegian) in order to improve translation quality of eTranslation, an online machine translation (MT) tool provided by the European Commission. The collected LRs were used for the development of neural MT engines in order to verify the quality of the resources. For all four languages, a total of 66 LRs were collected and made available on the ELRC-SHARE repository under various licenses. For Croatian, we have collected and published 20 LRs: 19 parallel corpora and 1 glossary. The majority of data is in the general domain (72 % of translation units), while the rest is in the eJustice (23 %), eHealth (3 %) and eProcurement (2 %) Digital Service Infrastructures (DSI) domains. The majority of the resources were for the Croatian-English language pair. The data was donated by six data contributors from the public as well as private sector. In this paper we present a subset of 13 Croatian LRs developed based on public administration documents, which are all made freely available, as well as challenges associated with the data collection, cleaning and processing.

Keywords: language resources, parallel corpora, machine translation, Connecting Europe Facility, eTranslation, PRINCIPLE

1. Introduction

PRINCIPLE[1] (*Providing Resources in Irish, Norwegian, Croatian and Icelandic for the Purposes of Language Engineering*) was a project funded by the Connecting Europe Facility (CEF) Telecom instrument[2], a project that focused on the identification, collection and processing of language resources (LRs) for four European under-resourced languages (Croatian, Icelandic, Irish and Norwegian) in order to improve translation quality of eTranslation[3], an online machine translation (MT) tool provided by the European Commission (EC). In this paper we present a freely available subset of Croatian LRs developed based on the public administration documents as well as challenges associated with the data collection, cleaning and processing.

The paper is structured as follows: Section 2 discusses the motivation for data collection as well as the objectives of the PRINCIPLE project within which the aforementioned activities took place, while Section 3 presents related work. Section 4 outlines the data collection process of all Croatian LRs with specific attention to the collection of public sector information. Section 5 describes the challenges of the data cleaning and processing we faced. In Section 6 we present statistics for 13 parallel corpora we have collected in three DSI domains (eJustice, eHealth, eProcurement) as well as in the general domain, followed by Section 7 with a conclusion.

2. Motivation and Objectives

In 2015 the EC, with its president at the time Jean-Clause Juncker, announced *A Digital Single Market Strategy for Europe*[4], identifying the Internet and digital technologies as an opportunity to contribute to the economy, create new jobs, and enhance Europe's position as a world leader in the digital economy which will contribute to the European digital transformation. The necessary EU digital transformation has been recognized by the von der Leyen Commission as well making *A Europe fit for the digital age* one of six priorities[5]. We can safely state that this transformation was abruptly accelerated in various social and economic sectors by the COVID-19 pandemic outbreak in 2020.

One way the EC supports the digital transformation and multilingualism is funding of the development of language technologies (resources and tools) of all its official languages as well as additional non-EU languages[6]. However, language technology support differs significantly between languages and language pair combinations. Rehm and Uszkoreit (2012) and Rehm et al. (2014) analyzed the state of language technology for 47 European languages investigating four categories: machine translation, speech processing, text analytics, and speech and text resources. Only the English language has good support in all four categories. All other languages have moderate support, fragmentary support or weak/no support, with the majority of the languages falling into the last category.

PRINCIPLE was a 2-year project (September 2019 - August 2021) funded by the CEF instrument, which focused on the identification, collection and processing of

1 https://principleproject.eu/

2 https://ec.europa.eu/inea/en/connecting-europe-facility/cef-telecom

3 https://ec.europa.eu/info/resources-partners/machine-translation-public-administrations-etranslation_en

4 The European Commision. Communication from the Commision to the European Parliament, the Council, the European Economic and Social Committee and the Committee of the Regions – A Digital Single Market Strategy for Europe. The European Commission : Brussels 2015. 192 final. URL: http://eur-lex.europa.eu/legal-content/EN/TXT/HTML/?uri=CELEX:52015DC0192&from=EN. (3 Jan 2022)

5 The European Commision. The European Commission's priorities. https://ec.europa.eu/info/strategy/priorities-2019-2024_en (3 Jan 2022)

6 For example Icelandic and Norwegian since Iceland and Norway are part of the European Free Trade Association (EFTA), which are part of the EU single market via the European Economic Area (EEA).

LRs for four European under-resourced languages: Croatian, Icelandic, Irish and Norwegian (covering both official varieties Bokmål and Nynorsk) (Way and Gaspari, 2019; Way et al., 2020). The Action was coordinated by Dublin City University, and involved the Faculty of Humanities and Social Sciences of the University of Zagreb, the National Library of Norway, the University of Iceland and Iconic Translation Machines Ltd. The main focus of the Action was on providing high-quality data in order to improve translation quality of eTranslation, an online MT tool provided by the EC, with a specific focus on two DSI domains: eJustice and eProcurement. Due to the COVID-19 pandemic outbreak, the focus was also extended to the eHealth DSI domain during the project duration. In order to verify the quality of the collected LRs, bespoke domain-adapted neural machine translation (NMT) engines were developed. The evaluations of the MT systems built as part of the project show significant improvements in BLEU scores on in-domain test datasets when using the collected project data. In-domain systems using our data outperform the best online systems by as much as 14.7 points (see Table 1). More details on building the NMT systems can be found in Moran et al. (2021). For all four languages, a total of 66 LRs were collected and made available on the ELRC-SHARE repository[7] under various licenses.

Engine	eProcurement	eJustice	eHealth
Iconic Engine	56.3	51.1	52.9
ONLINE1	49.1	37.9	38.2
ONLINE2	45.9	31.7	43.8

Table 1: SBLEU evaluations scores of the various in-domain engines built as part of the PRINCIPLE project.

In this paper we focus on our contribution to Croatian LRs. Based on the aforementioned cross-language comparison (Rehm and Uszkoreit 2012), the Croatian language has weak or no support in three categories: machine translation, speech processing and text analytics, and has fragmentary support for speech and text processing. In a recent overview of the European language technology landscape conducted by Rehm et al. (2020), it is revealed that still no national funding programs exist in Croatia despite Croatian being a technologically underdeveloped language.

As part of the PRINCIPLE Action activities, we have collected and published a total of 20 Croatian LRs, most of which contain the Croatian-English language pair: 19 parallel corpora and 1 glossary, all uploaded to the ELRC-SHARE repository. The majority of the data belongs to the general domain (72 % translation units [TUs]), while the rest belong to the eJustice (23 %), eHealth (3 %) and eProcurement (2 %) DSI domains. The data was donated by seven data contributors from the public and private sector.

In this paper we only provide a brief overview of the full set of Croatian LRs collected in the Action, and focus on 13 freely available Croatian LRs developed from public administration documents, as well as challenges associated with data collection, cleaning and processing.

3. Related Work

PRINCIPLE initially focused on building high-quality parallel corpora within the eJustice and eProcurement DSI domain. However, as a result of the COVID-19 disease pandemic outbreak, in the course of the project implementation, collection of language resources was extended to the eHealth DSI domain as well.

The ELRC-SHARE repository serves as a hub for "documenting, storing, browsing and accessing Language Resources that are collected through the European Language Resource Coordination and considered useful for feeding the CEF Automated Translation (CEF.AT) platform"[8]. An analysis of the repository reveals that out of 1416 parallel corpora, almost half are pertinent to the eHealth DSI domain (690 i.e. 49%). Out of those 690 parallel corpora, 636 (92%) were uploaded in 2020 or later, while only 54 (8%) were uploaded before the pandemic outbreak. The data has been collected from publicly available portals (e.g. Publications Office of the European Union[9], European Medicines Agency[10], portal[11] of the European Centre for Disease Prevention and Control[12], press corner of the EC, portal of the European Parliament[13], Wikipedia articles on regarding health and COVID-19 domain, etc.) as part of various projects financed by the EC (e.g. various iterations of the European Language Resource Coordination (ELRC)[14] and the Paracrawl[15] project, the EuroPat[16] project, the MaCoCu[17] project, etc.). The aforementioned projects produced the majority of the parallel corpora within the eJustice (396) and the eProcurement (358) DSI domains. In contrast with these previous projects which gathered publicly available data from readily available sources, the data collected as part of the PRINCIPLE project was not publicly available on portals of public administration bodies, but was scattered on their websites (unpaired

7 https://elrc-share.eu/
On the ELRC-SHARE repository there are two projects related to the PRINCIPLE Action: "PRINCIPLE - Unevaluated" and "PRINCIPLE - Evaluated". Unevaluated data corresponds to LRs that have been created by the project partners from documents donated by data providers. These LRs have been processed and cleaned either by the data providers themselves or by PRINCIPLE project partners, thus ensuring high quality. Evaluated data means that the LRs in question have been used by Iconic Translation Machines Ltd. to develop a range of state-of-the-art bespoke MT engines for early adopters, matching their specific use-cases. It should be noted that these LRs are a subset of the unevaluated LRs and have gone through additional processing, cleaning and evaluation steps.
PRINCIPLE - Unevaluated:
https://elrc-share.eu/repository/search/?q=&selected_facets=projectFilter_exact%3APRINCIPLE%20-%20Unevaluated.
PRINCIPLE - Evaluated:
https://elrc-share.eu/repository/search/?q=&selected_facets=projectFilter_exact%3APRINCIPLE%20-%20Evaluated.

8 https://elrc-share.eu/
9 https://op.europa.eu/en/home
10 https://www.ema.europa.eu/
11 https://antibiotic.ecdc.europa.eu/
12 https://www.ecdc.europa.eu/en
13 https://www.europarl.europa.eu/
14 https://www.lr-coordination.eu/
15 https://paracrawl.eu/
16 https://europat.net/
17 https://macocu.eu/

parallel documents), while some were not even publicly available.

In other related work, we acknowledge that there have been various endeavors applying diverse methods to collect corpora appropriate for MT engines. Here we present only a small selection of such works related to low-resourced language pairs and/or domains. Váradi et al. (2020) present the Croatian-English Parallel Corpus of Croatian National Legislation consisting of over 1,800 documents developed as part of the MARCELL[18] project. The English translations were exclusively in PDF format, hence the quality of automatic text extraction was diminished. Sentence alignment was performed automatically, and a manual inspection and correction was conducted. The corpus contains 396,984 TUs. Utka et al. (2022) present the English-Lithuanian comparable corpus DVITAS in the cybersecurity domain containing over 1,700 English and 2,500 Lithuaninan documents developed for the automatic bilingual term extraction. The corpus contains 4M words, 2M per language. Ghaddar and Langlais (2020) present a Large Scale French-English Financial Domain Parallel Corpus SEDAR in the low-resourced financial domain based on publicly available documents and information in PDF format. Due to this particular information being strictly forbidden to extract automatically, the authors describe the methodology they have applied for text extraction. The corpus contains 8.6 million high quality sentence pairs.

4. Data Collection

The data used for the development of Croatian LRs was donated by six data contributors from the public sector and one from the private sector:

- the Ministry of Foreign and European Affairs,
- the Central State Office for the Development of the Digital Society,
- the Central State Office for Central Public Procurement,
- the State Commission for Supervision of Public Procurement Procedures,
- the Faculty of Humanities and Social Sciences, University of Zagreb, and
- Ciklopea d.o.o.

The Ministry of Foreign and European Affairs donated documents in various formats (MS Word format, PDF format, TMX format, SDLTM format, HTML format) that were used for the development of five LRs in eJustice and eHealth DSI domains.

The Central State Office for the Development of the Digital Society donated documents in MS Word, PDF and HTML format that were used for the development of five LRs in the eProcurement and eJustice DSI domains, as well as the general domain.

The Central State Office for Central Public Procurement donated documents in MS Word format that were used for the development of two LRs in the eProcurement DSI domain.

The State Commission for Supervision of Public Procurement Procedures donated documents in MS Word format that were used in the development of three LRs in the eProcurement and eJustice DSI domains.

The Faculty of Humanities and Social Sciences University of Zagreb donated four resources. One resource was donated in TMX format in the eJustice DSI domain. The other three resources in the general domain were developed prior to the PRINCIPLE project and are in TXT format[19]. Those resources required acquiring permissions from their developers to use the data for improving the eTranslation system. All four resources from the Faculty of Humanities and Social Sciences did not require any additional processing, and are excluded from further LR descriptions.

Ciklopea d.o.o., a translation and localization company, cleaned, processed and/or anonymized all data themselves before donating it to the PRINCIPLE project in TMX format. The only additional processing that was done on their data was during the development of bespoke NMT engines. Three LRs were developed based on data Ciklopea d.o.o. donated, which are not included in further LR descriptions.

We had contacted additional public sector institutions to the ones mentioned above, but were not successful in establishing collaboration. Based on the experiences of successful and unsuccessful collaborations with the public administrations, we have identified the following main challenges in collecting data for the development of parallel corpora from such institutions. a) Identifying what public sector institutions and departments produce parallel documents in two or more languages since the majority of documentation is produced in either Croatian or in other languages directly without a Croatian equivalent. b) Pairing of parallel documents since the majority are scattered over different departments and/or on various computers. c) Bureaucracy since sharing of some documents needed to be subjected to complex internal protocols. d) Intellectual property concerns since it was unclear who was the owner of the content, specifically for translations that were outsourced. e) Privacy concerns since some data contain sensitive information, and unwillingness to share the data for anonymization. f) Shortage of manpower since consolidating the data prior to donating is time consuming and not part of the provider's regular workflow.

5. Data Cleaning and Processing

One of our aims was to normalize the collected data and to generate resources in a unified format which would be suited for MT system development. Hence, the end goal of the data cleaning and processing was a sentence-aligned corpus in TXT format[20]. Given the variety of

18 https://marcell-project.eu

19 The following previously developed resources have been uploaded to the ELRC-SHARE repository:
- SETimes parallel corpus (Agić and Ljubešić, 2014) https://opus.nlpl.eu/SETIMES.php
- hrenWaC (Ljubešić et al., 2016) https://opus.nlpl.eu/hrenWaC.php
- hrenWaC 2.0 https://www.clarin.si/repository/xmlui/handle/11356/1058.

20 Note that some data providers handed over data in TMX format which was already manually aligned at the TU level. Upon inspection, these units were often sentences, but sometimes also comprised smaller or greater units. We uploaded

formats the data was originally provided in, we had to implement a number of processing steps to obtain the desired format.

5.1 Text Extraction

In principle, documents formatted in HTML and MS Word format proved easier to work with in comparison with the PDF format. For the former, we inspected the contents and manually copied the text into plain text files, while making interventions on two fronts: a) when parts of a document were missing or untranslated, we removed those sections to minimize alignment problems, and b) we did not incorporate all the text from tables, picture descriptions and formulas found in documents containing annual reports or financial statements which included a large amount of numerical data with little to no useful language data.

When it comes to the PDF documents, many contained selectable text, while others were simple scans of original documents where text could not be extracted. Due to this, the extraction from PDF documents was both done manually and using optical character recognition (OCR) software[21] where needed. When manually extracting content, we followed the same guidelines as for HTML and MS Word documents. Extracting footnotes presented additional issues for both manual and OCR data extraction: as sentences do not always end at the bottom of a page, footnote extraction had to be supervised in order not to split sentences and paragraphs.

The majority of the bilingual data was provided as two separate documents, one for each language, however some documents came as two-column PDFs in which each column represents one of the languages. Naturally, we had to split these documents into parallel monolingual TXT files. The processing of these PDF documents proved to be the most time-consuming task, as no straightforward automated solution was available. In addition, some of the PDF documents were not formatted correctly, so we had to handle them with particular diligence.

5.2 Data Cleaning

Upon extracting the text into TXT files, we had to additionally clean the data to improve its quality, as some of the provided data was noisy to begin with, and using OCR introduced additional noise. Certain issues were encountered across the board: there were unnecessary parts of the text (e.g. point strings and page number tags in the content), boilerplate content was frequently repeated, sentences were broken into multiple lines, bullets into separate lines, etc. Other issues were specific to OCR: incorrect recognition of diacritics found in English texts (e.g. *Zavižan* was recognized as *Zavizan*), incorrect recognition of letters in Croatian texts (e.g. the letter *đ* was recognized as *d*), appearance of the ¬ sign inside of words, tabs instead of spaces, whitespace gaps, etc. A bigger problem was when two words were joined together, as this could not be detected automatically. This means that every document was skim-read to detect words that were joined. Additionally, words that had a footnote label next to them were often combined with the footnote number (e.g. *Hrvatske3*), and it was even more complicated when the footnote number was combined with, for example, a year or other numerical data. Tables also required special attention: each table was manually checked in case it happened to split a sentence into two parts, or in case multiple columns of one row were merged.

One of the most interesting errors that occurred only in some of the searchable PDFs are ligatures: a product of a particular text font connecting or merging two letters into one letter, resulting in spacing errors when the text is copied from the PDF. Connecting letters with ligatures usually happens when the capital 'T' is followed by the letter 'h' which appears in frequent English words such as: *Th is*, *Th ey*, *Th e*. The other common case in which ligatures appear are words with the letter 'f' followed by letters such as 'i', 'l', 'f'. Examples include: *profi l*, *fi ltar*, *jeft iniji*, *Direzione Aff ari Internazionali*. Their frequency in both Croatian and English was considerable, but the list of affected strings was finite. This allowed us to identify all ligature sequences that occur in the texts, and then group them into categories based on whether they can be corrected automatically or not, which facilitated a straightforward cleaning process. The sequences were categorized as follows: a) the sequence is a ligature in both Croatian and English documents, b) the sequence is a ligature only in Croatian documents, c) the sequence is a ligature only in English documents, and d) the sequence has to be checked manually for every single match.

Alongside PDFs, there was considerable noise in some of the HTML documents, but the errors were more often related to individual words than to structural issues. The use of regular expressions proved effective in finding the errors, but not in their automatic correction. For example, a common mistake was the combination of a dot and a word, i.e. the dot was either in front of the first letter (e.g. *.treaty*) or inside the word (e.g. *implementa.tion*). Furthermore, letters with diacritics appearing within English words, e.g. *Condžttidžns*, were also somewhat challenging. Croatian texts exhibited similar phenomena: *meQutim* instead of *međutim*, *me8unarodne* instead of *međunarodne*, etc. The biggest problem with such errors is that not all combinations could be found and almost every document had its own specific examples.

Finally, once all cleaning was completed, we used a sentence aligner to align the parallel documents at the sentence level. Specifically, we used vecalign (Thompson and Koehn, 2019), a state of the art automatic alignment tool that uses fastText embeddings (Grave et al., 2018) to calculate the alignments of the TUs[22] in our processed corpora. In terms of parameters, we set the maximum number of allowed overlaps to 5, maximum alignment size to 4, and during embedding training we used the provided English tokenizer for the English side of the corpus, while we used the provided Slovene tokenizer for the Croatian side of the corpus, as a Croatian tokenizer was not provided in vecalign's pipeline. As expected, this

them as is, foregoing automatic alignment, as they already satisfy the required format and can be considered gold-standard.

21 We used the commercial ABBYY Finereader OCR software. https://www.abbyy.com

22 Note that while none of the TUs in these datasets are larger than a single sentence, they can be smaller, as they sometimes contain text segments like list entries, table cell content, section titles or subtitles, which are often not complete sentences and can be as short as a single word or phrase.

did not seem to cause any issues, likely due to the high similarity between Slovene and Croatian. After performing the alignment we manually checked a random subsample of aligned sentence pairs to confirm the tool's accuracy. On 100 randomly sampled sentence pairs, 98 were accurately aligned. This high accuracy is likely due to the fact that the parallel data was extensively preprocessed and was well-prepared for automatic alignment. Any incorrect translation pairs are more likely to be a consequence of noise in the parallel documents, rather than a mistake of the alignment tool itself.

6. Corpora Statistics

After completing the processing steps the resources were ready for publication. Here we present an overview of the 13 resources categorized by domain. Cumulative descriptive statistics per domain are provided in Table 2. All resources contain at least the Croatian-English pair.

Domain	TUs
eJustice	738,923 (88.71 %)
eProcurement	22,703 (2.73 %)
eHealth	563 (0.07 %)
General	70,810 (8,5 %)
Total	*832,999*

Table 2: Translation unit (TU) counts for the 13 corpora as grouped by DSI domains.

6.1 eJustice Domain

Eight resources belong to the eJustice domain, seven of which are parallel corpora, while one is a glossary of legal terms. In addition to the Croatian-English language pair present in all the resources, the glossary also contains translations in German. One of the resources has been additionally filtered and evaluated via an MT development pipeline. They were provided by 4 different data providers: Croatian Ministry of Foreign and European Affairs, the State Commission for Supervision of Public Procurement Procedures, the Central State Office for the Development of the Digital Society and the Faculty of Humanities and Social Sciences, University of Zagreb. As such, they contain a variety of legal documents, EU court judgements and international agreements and are all freely available, totalling 738,923 TUs (see Table 3).

6.2 eProcurement Domain

There are 3 parallel corpora belonging to the eProcurement domain, each donated by a different data provider: the Central State Office for the Development of the Digital Society, the State Commission for Supervision of Public Procurement Procedures and the Central Public Procurement Office. They contain a variety of public procurement documents, including directives of the European Parliament and of the Council. In total, they contain 22,703 TUs (see Table 4).

6.3 eHealth Domain

There is one parallel corpus belonging to the eHealth domain. It was donated by the Croatian Ministry of Foreign and European Affairs and contains decisions related to the COVID-19 disease pandemic. It contains 563 TUs (see Table 5).

6.4 General Domain

The remaining parallel corpus belongs to the General domain. It was donated by the Central State Office for the Development of the Digital Society and contains a wide variety of documents on a mixture of topics such as newsletters, tax regulations, science and statistical information. It contains 70,810 TUs (see Table 6).

Corpus name	TUs
PRINCIPLE MVEP Croatian-English-German Glossary of Legal Terms	1,485
PRINCIPLE DKOM Croatian-English Parallel Corpus of legal documents	492
PRINCIPLE MVEP Croatian-English Parallel Corpus of legal documents	113,685
PRINCIPLE MVEP Croatian-English Parallel Corpus in the legal domain (evaluated)	110,649
PRINCIPLE MVEP Croatian-English Parallel Corpus of Court Judgements	13,335
PRINCIPLE SDURDD Croatian-English Parallel Corpus in the legal domain	261,046
PRINCIPLE SDURDD Croatian-English Parallel Corpus of international agreements	234,500
PRINCIPLE FFZG Croatian-English Parallel Corpus in the eJustice domain	3,731

Table 3: Translation unit (TU) counts for the 8 resources belonging to the eJustice domain.

Corpus name	TUs
PRINCIPLE SDURDD Croatian-English Procurement Parallel Corpus	3,911
PRINCIPLE DKOM Croatian-English Parallel Corpus of Directives of the European Parliament and of the Council	11,511
PRINCIPLE Central Public Procurement Office of Republic of Croatia Croatian-English Procurement Parallel Corpus	7,281

Table 4: Translation unit (TU) counts for the 3 resources belonging to the eProcurement domain.

Corpus name	TUs
PRINCIPLE MVEP Croatian-English Parallel Corpus of Decisions related to the COVID-19 disease epidemic	563

Table 5: Translation unit (TU) counts for the resources belonging to the eHealth domain.

Corpus name	TUs
PRINCIPLE SDURDD Croatian-English Parallel Corpus in the General Domain	70,810

Table 6: Translation unit (TU) counts for the resources belonging to the General domain.

7. Conclusion

As a result of the CEF-funded project PRINCIPLE, a total of 20 distinct Croatian LRs have been developed: 19 parallel corpora and 1 glossary. All LRs are uploaded to the ELRC-SHARE repository under various licenses, and many are freely available. We believe we have made a substantial contribution to the improvement of the Croatian-English language pair in the eTranslations system in two DSI domains. On the ELRC-SHARE repository at the time Croatian LRs were contributed (May 2021), 5 (26 %) out of 19 Croatian LRs were in the eProcurement domain and 10 (34 %) out of 29 were in the eJustice domain. We have made a moderate contribution to the eHealth domain by uploading 3 (6 %) out of 49 Croatian LRs.

In this paper we presented 13 freely available LRs developed from data donated by six data contributors from the public administration, and presented the particular challenges associated with data collection, cleaning and processing. The LRs cover three DSI domains (eJustice, eProcurement and eHealth) as well as data in the general domain, sizing in total 832,999 TUs. In order to continuously collect public administration data and develop LRs from this data, it would be beneficial for the Croatian language to have data donation processes incorporated into workflows of data creators. However, language data collection has not been identified as a priority in Croatia, as there is no infrastructure or (financial) support on the national level that would serve as a hub for collection and processing of language resources and tools as well as a center for educating stakeholders interested in contributing, developing and/or using Croatian language technologies.

8. Acknowledgements

PRINCIPLE was generously co-financed by the European Union Connecting Europe Facility under Action 2018-EU-IA-0050 with grant agreement INEA/CEF/ICT/A2018/1761837. We wish to thank all our data providers for donating their valuable time and data, as well as all our colleagues and students who contributed to the project. This paper was written with the financial support of Science Foundation Ireland under Grant Agreement No. 13/RC/2106_P2 at the ADAPT SFI Research Centre at Technological University Dublin. ADAPT, the SFI Research Centre for AI-Driven Digital Content Technology, is funded by Science Foundation Ireland through the SFI Research Centres Programme. We thank the anonymous reviewers for their insightful comments.

9. Bibliographical References

Agić, Ž and Ljubešić, N. (2014). The SETimes.HR Linguistically Annotated Corpus of Croatian. *Proceedings of the Ninth International Conference on Language Resources and Evaluation (LREC' 2014)* (pp. 1724-1727).

Ghaddar, A., & Langlais, P. (2020). SEDAR: a Large Scale French-English Financial Domain Parallel Corpus. In *Proceedings of the 12th Language Resources and Evaluation Conference (LREC 2020)* (pp. 3595-3602).

Grave, E., Bojanowski, P., Gupta, P., Joulin, A., Mikolov, T. (2018). Learning Word Vectors for 157 Languages. In *Proceedings of the International Conference on Language Resources and Evaluation (LREC 2018)* (pp. 3483-3487).

Ljubešić, N., Esplà-Gomis, M, Toral, A.,Ortiz Rojas, S., Klubička, F. Producing Monolingual and Parallel Web Corpora at the Same Time - SpiderLing and Bitextor's Love Affair. *Proceedings of the Tenth International Conference on Language Resources and Evaluation (LREC 2016)* (pp. 2949-2956).

Moran, R., Escartín, C. P., Ramesh, A., Sheridan, P., Dunne, J., Gaspari, F., Castilho, S., Resende, N. and Way, A. (2021). Building MT systems in low resourced languages for Public Sector users in Croatia, Iceland, Ireland, and Norway. In *Proceedings of Machine Translation Summit XVIII: Users and Providers Track* (pp. 353-381).

Rehm, G., Marheinecke, K., Hegele, S., Piperidis, S., Bontcheva, K., Hajič, J., Choukri, K., Vasiļjevs, A., Backfried, G., Prinz, C., Gómez Pérez, J. M., Meertens, L., Lukowicz, P., van Genabith, J., Lösch, A., Slusallek, P., Irgens, M., Gatellier, P., Köhler, J., Le Bars, L., Anastasiou, D., Auksoriūtė, A., Bel, N., Branco, A., Budin, G., Daelemans, W., De Smedt, K., Garabík, R., Gavriilidou, M., Gromann, D., Koeva, S., Krek, S., Krstev, C., Lindén, K., Magnini, B., Odijk, J., Ogrodniczuk, M., Rögnvaldsson, E., Rosner, M., Sandford Pedersen, B., Skadiņa, I., Tadić, M., Tufiş, D., Váradi, T., Vider, K., Way, A., and Yvon, F. (2020). The European Language Technology Landscape in 2020: Language-Centric and Human-Centric AI for Cross-Cultural Communication in Multilingual Europe. In *Proceedings of the 12th Language Resources and Evaluation Conference (LREC 2020)* (pp. 3322-3332).

Rehm, G. and Uszkoreit, H., editors. (2012). META-NET White Paper Series: Key Results and Cross-Language Comparison. *META-NET White Paper Series. Kaiserslautern: Deutsches Forschungszentrum für Künstliche Intelligenz (DFKI). https://web. archive. org/web/20181219124131/http://www. meta-net. eu/whitepapers/key-results-and-cross-language-comparison (13.12. 2018)*.

Rehm, G., Uszkoreit, H., Dagan, I., Goetcherian, V., Dogan, M. U., and Váradi, T. (2014). An update and extension of the META-NET Study "Europe's Languages in the digital age".

Thompson, B. and Koehn, P., 2019, November. Vecalign: Improved sentence alignment in linear time and space. In *Proceedings of the 2019 Conference on Empirical Methods in Natural Language Processing and the 9th International Joint Conference on Natural Language Processing (EMNLP-IJCNLP)* (pp. 1342-1348).

Utka, Andrius; Rackevičienė, Sigita; Rokas, Aivaras; Bielinskienė, Agnė; Mockienė, Liudmila and Laurinaitis, Marius, 2022, *English-Lithuanian Comparable Cybersecurity Corpus - DVITAS*, CLARIN-LT digital library in the Republic of Lithuania, http://hdl.handle.net/20.500.11821/47.

Váradi, T., Koeva, S., Yalamov, M., Tadić, M., Sass, B., & Nitoń, B. (2020). The MARCELL Legislative Corpus. In *Proceedings of the International Conference on Language Resources and Evaluation (LREC 2020)* (pp. 3761-3768).

Way, A, Bago, P, Dunne, J., Gaspari, F., Kåsen, A., Kristmannson, G., McHugh, H., Olsen, J. A., Sheridan, D. D., Sheridan, P., Tinsley, J. (2020.) Progress of the PRINCIPLE Project: Promoting MT for Croatian, Icelandic, Irish and Norwegian. In *Proceedings of the 22nd Annual Conference of the European Association for Machine Translation* (pp. 465-466).

Way, A., Gaspari, F. (2019). PRINCIPLE: Providing Resources in Irish, Norwegian, Croatian and Icelandic for the Purposes of Language Engineering. In *Proceedings of MT Summit XVII, volume 2* (pp. 112-113).

Proceedings of the 15th Workshop on Building and Using Comparable Corpora (BUCC 2022) @LREC2022 , pages 56–60
Marseille, June 25, 2022
© European Language Resources Association (ELRA), licensed under CC-BY-NC

Setting Up Bilingual Comparable Corpora with Non-Contemporary Languages

Helena Bermúdez Sabel, Francesca Dell'Oro, Cyrielle Montrichard, Corinne Rossari
University of Neuchâtel
2000 Neuchatel (Switzerland)
{helena.bermudez, francesca.delloro, cyrielle.montrichard, corinne.rossari}@unine.ch

Abstract

This paper presents the project *Les corpora latins et français: une fabrique pour l'accès à la représentation des connaissances (Latin and French Corpora: a Factory for Accessing Knowledge Representation*) whose focus is the study of modality in both Latin and French by means of multi-genre, diachronic comparable corpora. The setting up of such corpora involves a number of conceptualisation challenges, in particular with regard to how to compare two asynchronous textual productions corresponding to different cultural frameworks. In this paper we outline the rationale of designing comparable corpora to explore our research questions and then focus on some of the issues that arise when comparing different diachronic spans of Latin and French. We also explain how these issues were dealt with, thus providing some grounds upon which other projects could build their methodology.

Keywords: comparability of language stages, genres, modality, annotation

1. Introduction

The project *Les corpora latins et français: une fabrique pour l'accès à la représentation des connaissances* (*Latin and French Corpora: a Factory for Accessing Knowledge Representation*), which started in February 2022, aims at comparing the use of modality in two languages which have a filiation relation: Latin and French. By the term 'modality' we refer to the linguistic expression of the stance of the speaker towards the propositional content of an utterance (Nuyts, 2005).

This project stems from the empirical observation of the variety of markers showing the speaker's stance in different languages (Narrog, 2016, Boye, 2016). Choosing two languages that are temporally distant, but genetically connected, enables us to pinpoint the continuity and the discontinuity in the usage of modal forms. We have thus to deal with textual productions belonging to different chronologies, which is not usually the case when speaking of comparable corpora[1] (for an exception, however, cf. van der Auwera and Diewald, 2012). To manage this issue, we needed to elaborate a dedicated methodology and set up corpora that could be compared as being representative samples of selected language stages. To this end, we took into account two different chronologic spans (according to traditional periodisations) for each of the two languages: Classical Latin (1st BCE to 3rd CE) and Early Mediaeval Latin (6th CE to 9th CE), and Classical French (1650-1799) and Modern French (1800-1979), respectively. Then, we set up the four corpora based on the selection of comparable genres in the two languages and in the four spans, though the notion of 'comparable genres' is a challenging one, when dealing with several asynchronous stages. Moreover, as one of our goals is also that of applying statistical methods to study the corpus, a major difficulty lies in comparing linguistic stages that involve each a different grammatical, orthographic and morphosyntactic evolution.

In this paper we outline our methodology to set up comparable corpora in Latin and French considering time period, genres and logistical means such as the availability of texts (especially in Latin). First, we describe the goals of our ongoing project and its aims, specifically considering its stumbling blocks. Then, we outline the choices we made to achieve the setting up of the corpora. Finally, we present how we devised to deal with different annotation tagsets and how those choices allow us to compare the two languages in a tool-based linguistic approach.

2. Studying and Comparing Modality Markers in Latin and French

2.1 Main Goals of the Project

The goal of the project is to identify the markers of modality, such as morphological or lexical devices and their uses, in the two languages, while taking into account the different genres (informative, ordinary writing, legal, among others) at different historical stages. After having collected the data, the obtained results will be compared in order to measure the similarities and differences in the use of the markers in terms of their presence/absence, their frequency (specificity score) and their association properties (co-occurrence specificity score). In order to do so, we plan to use textometric tools and specifically TXM[2] (Heiden, 2010). This is a platform that provides statistical tools (co-occurrence specificity score, specificity score, factorial correspondence analysis etc.), annotation tools (Heiden, 2018) and an easy access to the full text or to the view of keywords in context.

As mentioned above, the aim of the project is twofold: comparing modality in Latin and French and, at the same time, looking at the differences due to discourse genres in each language and between the two languages. The underlying methodology which mixes chronological spans and discourse genres, is particularly relevant for modality, whose values are instable, but it is efficient for any linguistic enquiry, since it allows one to better evaluate which linguistic elements are genre-dependent and which ones are specific to a particular period. The results of this

[1] See, for example, the catalogue of comparable corpora available at the Virtual Language Observatory (CLARIN 2021).

[2] Link to the website project: https://txm.gitpages.huma-num.fr/textometrie/en/

analysis could be easily extrapolated for analysing other Romance languages. These corpora will be made freely available to the scientific community under a Creative Commons license. Our corpora will facilitate the exploration of different research questions involving a contrastive perspective, and the semantic annotation can be exploited for studies that are adjacent to modality (e.g. enunciative responsibility).

2.2 Some Challenges of Building Asynchronous Comparable Corpora

The definitions given of comparable corpora in the literature and specifically in Corpus Linguistics (Sinclair, 1996; Habert et al., 1997, Talvensaari et al., 2007) are often vague and based on stressing the differences between comparable and parallel corpora.[3] Comparable corpora are thus defined as corpora built with texts in more than one language, with a purpose of comparison and with at least a common point represented by style and/or topics. However, some scholars also point out another required common point: the same time period (Kontonatsios, 2015: 38; McEnery, 2003: 450). Cf. the following list of relevant points for setting up comparable corpora:

> "the parameters that need to be controlled in order to compare languages include:
> – the time when the texts were written;
> – their discursive genre (descriptive, argumentative, etc.);
> – the type of audience targeted and their field (law, science, etc.)." (Zufferey, 2020: 83)

It is important to stress that this view is strictly dependent on a synchronic approach to text corpora. In fact, as shown by van der Auwera and Diewald (2012) comparable corpora can also consist of texts pertaining to distant diachronic spans.

Concerning the other criteria, it seems to us that the ones suggested by Zufferey (2020) are more precise than the notions of 'style' or 'topics' usually used. In fact, the latest may turn out to be problematic when selecting the relevant texts. For instance, a medical topic can be treated very differently according to the type of text and the period (written press, a filmed documentary, academic papers, scientific magazines, etc.). With regard to the audience in the past centuries, we cannot know it with precision. Therefore, this criterion is not applicable in the case of our corpora. Thus, genre and domain become the only suitable criteria for building our comparable corpora.

With reference to the setting up of our corpus, the following issues emerged:

(i) the difference in the time period inherent in our corpus: the two languages are not used simultaneously over time (at least not by native speakers);

(ii) genres are subject to variation over time and this complicates the possibility to compare works from different time spans.

However, we believe that it is possible to work around these two challenges in order to achieve our goal without disregarding them, and thus find a workable solution—maybe an imperfect one, but as Habert et al. put it (1997), working on imperfect data is the only way to contribute to corpus linguistics.[4]

We needed to devise a methodology for the selection of texts in order to master the intrinsic features of the data and the corpora. In the next section we outline such methodology and how we elaborated it.

3. Methodology for the Selection of Texts and Related Issues

3.1 Building a Corpus to Answer Our Research Questions

It is worth stressing that we adhere to the assertion by Hunston (2002) that a corpus is mainly a tool built in order to explore a research question. Many projects using comparable corpora focus on translation and terminology studies in order to create lexicons and translation resources when parallel corpora are not available (e.g. Delpech et al., 2012; Daille and Harastani, 2013) Our research is slightly different because it does not aim at studying how a modality marker is realised in both languages, but at observing the relations between the use of modality in a language and in one of its descendant languages. In particular, we want to assess which trends with regard to modality are due to diachrony and which ones are due to the genre. Both these questions are very important in the field of linguistics, in particular when analysing semantic change: for instance, it is relevant to take into account the notion of 'post-modality' in order to determine the diachronic evolution of the polysemy of modal markers (such as morphological markers or verbs, e.g. Latin *possum* and French *pouvoir* 'can').

3.2 Tackling Temporal Distance

As it is known, French and Latin coexisted during the Middle Ages, though Latin gradually ceased to be the mother tongue of any speaker. Our purpose is to isolate features concerning the use of modality in each language independently of the influence of one language on the other, but drawing on native or native-like speakers. Thus, contact influences between both linguistics systems generate interferences that go against the goals of the project as explained before. This is the reason why we decided to study diachronic spans for each language that do not overlap. In that way, we can take a look at the modal meaning conveyed by a marker in both languages at different time periods. Drawing on this, we will be able to

---

[3] See McEnery & Xiao (2007: 19 ff) for a discussion of terminological issues concerning parallel and comparable corpora and for a comprehensive definition of the latest term.

[4] "Les linguistiques de corpus se révèleront fructueuses comme domaine de recherche si l'on accepte l'imparfait, c'est-à-dire des ressources toujours « impures » [...] ". (Habert et. al., 1997: in Chapter X, section 2.3). Our translation: "Corpus linguistics will prove to be a fruitful field of research if we accept the imperfect, that is always 'impure' resources".

create a cartography of modality markers in both languages and see what is relevant in a certain time period and what seems to be subject to variation over time.

This particularity of our research allows us to pinpoint diachronic and cultural differences that go beyond topic or style. Since genres have an impact on the way of saying as shown in Pincemin & Rastier (1999) and Adam (1997), they have more weight in our selection criteria than topic. Such a choice is particularly suitable for our research question, as we are interested in how events are modalised, i.e. how they are presented: the event itself being not relevant.

3.3 Dealing with the Audience Criteria and Genre Variation

The parameters of genre should be considered simultaneously to the one of audience target because they are strictly interrelated. In fact, it is really complicated to dissociate, e.g. the genre 'academic paper' from the target audience of the genre.

For our work, we face a double constraint, i.e. (i) finding the 'same' genres attested over the centuries and (ii) finding inside those genres domains that can be compared. For instance, the genre of treaty is attested over time, but the subjects did evolve. Therefore, it is nowadays rare to encounter treaties about mystic topics and conversely to find treaties about communication media in Antiquity.

Moreover, it seems that genres, topics and audience show a great variation which could be related to the digital revolution. This has been documented, among other, by Paveau (2013). She proposes the term 'technogenre' and the following description:

> Ces technogenres sont des aménagements de genres préexistants (en twitterature en particulier) ou des inventions de l'écosystème numérique (Paveau, 2013: 24).
>
> These technogenres are adaptations of pre-existing genres (in twitterature in particular) or inventions of the digital ecosystem (our translation).

Among the variation and the creation of new genres, the 'digital ecosystem' led to the slow mutation of canonical genre such as the genre of correspondence which today could include emails or chats. Moreover, it is by far more difficult to delimit the target audience when the text is intended for the World Wide Web. This was for us the main reason for excluding the 20th and 21st centuries, thus excluding the modern stage of French language.

Second, as we considered it important to take into account the genre variation within a language through centuries, we decided to sample the Latin corpus and the French corpus at different time periods. The result gives us an original comparable corpus with multiple variables.

We propose to summarise what said above in the following schema (see Figure 1). The image shows a timeline in centuries, in which the selection of texts by time period, and genre is represented for each language (coded by different colours).

Figure 1 shows the macro-categories relevant for studying and comparing Latin and French: we separate technical treatises from literary genres and we keep a third category (Other) to include other function-specific genres such as correspondence or legal texts. Each one of these categories is further divided in sub-categories. For instance, technical treatises are grouped by domain: rhetoric and linguistics; philosophy; natural sciences. As an example, in the sub-category 'rhetoric and linguistics' we consider that the Latin works *De verborum significatione fragmentum* by Sextus Pompeius Festus (2nd CE) and *Ars grammatica* by Alcuinus (8th CE) are comparable to the *Grammaire universelle* by Court de Gébelin (1774) and the *Essai de sémantique: science des significations* by Michel Bréal (1887). Each sub-category is between 300'000 and 800'000 words long depending on texts availability (obviously, for Latin we have certain limitations concerning the number of works preserved for certain domains and their availability as free resources).

Figure 1 shows the different variables contained in our comparable corpora that will be exploited to investigate modality: it allows us to compare languages, genres, diachronic spans independently or in combination.

4. The Annotation Tagset

4.1 Automatic Lemmatisation and Part-of-Speech Tagging

For reasons of feasibility, we decided to carry out an automatic linguistic annotation of the corpora. As figure 1 shows, we retrieved texts in both languages from different chronological stages. One of the issues that arise from this is tied to the graphical representation of data. For instance, in Classical French verbs do not present the same endings. For example, the various forms of *devoir* 'must, have to' in Classical French do not have the same graphical representation as in Modern French, when the verb is conjugated. Similarly, Early Mediaeval Latin can display more recent variants with respect to Classical Latin. In order for us to avoid working based on graphic forms, which are very likely to change over time, we need to annotate our corpora and work with units that are less likely to change, i.e. lemma and morphosyntactic categories.

In order to obtain the best performance with regard to the automatic annotation, we are not only implementing language-specific annotation models, but also period specific models. We selected the following three morphosyntactic taggers:

- Treetagger and the annotation dataset for contemporary French
- Presto, an annotation dataset for Classical French designed during the implementation of the PRESTO project (Blumenthal and Vigier, 2018)
- Treetagger with the model trained by Gabriele Brandolini for Latin.

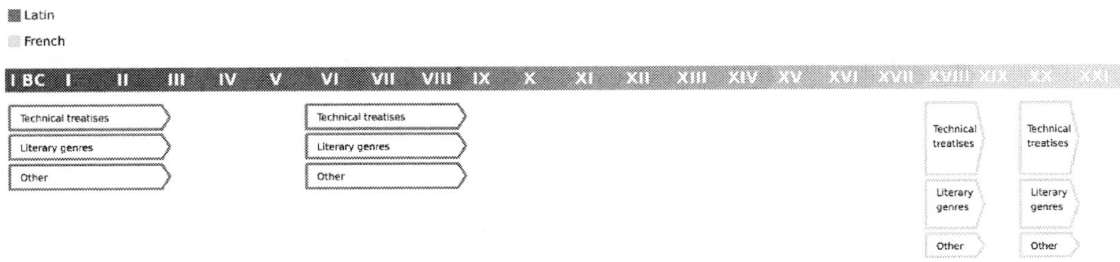

Figure 1. Graphic representation of the linguistic variables present in the project (language, genre, period)

For the various stages of French, there are differences not only at the level of the tagset, but also in the achieved precision. In Classical French we have pieces of information with tags about the subject of the verb according to its conjugation which is not available for Contemporary French. In order to solve this problem, we decided to keep the simplest tagging available, since it would be too time consuming to add a large number of tags.

4.2 Semi-automatic Semantic Annotation

As the main goal of our project is the study of modality, we devised an annotation tagset for the manual semantic annotation of modal markers that is appropriate for both languages and for the four linguistic stages of our corpora. We distinguish two major categories[5] (presented in Table 1 as well) of modality—epistemic and non-epistemic—with different sub-categories for each major category:

- epistemic: from weak degree of certainty (*Someone knocks on the door, this may well be the neighbour*) to strong degree of certainty (*Someone knocks on the door, this must be the neighbour)*
- non-epistemic: e.g.
  - capacity (*I can sing very well)*
  - generic possibility[6] (*The tennis court is free, we can go play*)
  - permission/obligation (*You must/may go now*)
  - volition (*I want to go to the movies*)

We devised two possible annotation procedures. As shown in Table 1, a marker which always conveys the same type of modality—e.g. French *peut-être* or Latin *forsitan* 'maybe' which express medium epistemic modality—allows a semi-automatic annotation within the TXM platform (making it possible to annotate at once every occurrence of a lemma). In the case of polyfunctional markers, such as French *pouvoir* and Latin *possum* 'can, to be able' which can express different types of modality—e.g. someone's ability to do something or an epistemic stance— we sample each corpus in order to manually annotate every occurrence of the term according to the type of modality it carries.

Major modality type	Examples of modal markers that can be semi-automatically annotated	Modal markers that required a manual annotation (meaning is context-dependant)
epistemic	FR: *certainement / probablement* LA*: forte*	FR: *pouvoir* LA: *possum* Both : morphological markers such as subjunctive/conditional affixes
non-epistemic	FR: *vouloir, obligatoirement, nécessairement* *LA: volo*	FR: *pouvoir/ devoir/ falloir* LA: *possum / debeo* FR : / *falloir* LA: *licet* Both: morphological markers such as future affixes

Table 1. Example of the annotation of some modal markers by type of modality

5. Conclusions

In order to achieve our goals and answer our research questions, we had to set up a methodology of selection and processing of texts for both Latin and French to assure the comparability of the corpora.

Our project is still at an early stage of its implementation. The corpora are not set up yet, but a methodology tackling the main challenges and tailored to our research goals has been defined.

This paper shows the different steps in elaborating our methodology concerning the selection and processing of texts. Its interest lays on the lack of documented endeavours working with diachronic comparable corpora.

6. Acknowledgements

This work is supported by the Empiris Foundation (fund *Jakob Wüest*).

[5] The definition of the main categories of modality is a debated subject. Our categorization is based on the distinction between epistemic modality and non-epistemic modality which is the most agreed upon.

[6] We distinguish generic possibility from epistemic modality: the latter corresponds to propositional modality and the former to event modality (Palmer, 2001).

7. Bibliographical References

Adam, J.-M. (1997). Genres, textes, discours : pour une reconception linguistique du concept de genre. In *Revue belge de philologie et d'histoire*, 75-3. pp. 665-681

Auwera van der, J. and Diewald, G. (2012). Methods for Modalities. In A. Ender et al. (Eds). *Methods in Contemporary Linguistics*. De Gruyter, pp. 121–142.

Blumenthal, P. and Vigier, D. (2018). Présentation. In P. Blumenthal & D. Vigier (Eds.). *Études diachroniques du français et perspectives sociétales*. Peter Lang, pp.7-20.

Boye, K. (2016). The Expression of Epistemic Modality. In J. Nuyts & J. van der Auwera (Eds.). *The Oxford Handbook of Modality and Mood*. Oxford University Press, Oxford, pp. 117–140.

Daille, B., and Harastani, R. (2013). TTC TermSuite - Terminological Alignment from Comparable Corpora (TTC TermSuite Alignement Terminologique à Partir de Corpus Comparables) [in French]. In *Proceedings of TALN 2013 (Volume 3 System Demonstrations)*, pages 812–813. Les Sables d'Olonne, France: ATALA.

Delpech, E., Daille, B., Morin, E. and Lemaire, C. (2012). Identification of Fertile Translations in Comparable Corpora: A Morpho-Compositional Approach. In *Proceedings of the 10th Conference of the Association for Machine Translation in the Americas: Research Papers*, [online], San Diego, California, USA: Association for Machine Translation in the Americas. https://aclanthology.org/2012.amta-papers.5.

Habert, B., Nazarenko, A. and Salem, A. (1997). Les linguistiques de corpus. Armand Colin, Paris. [online]. http://lexicometrica.univ-paris3.fr/livre/les_linguistiques_de_corpus_1997/

Heiden S. (2010). The TXM Platform: Building Open-Source Textual Analysis Software Compatible with the TEI Encoding Scheme. In *24th Pacific Asia Conference on Language, Information and Computation,* [online]. Sendai, Japan. http://halshs.archives-ouvertes.fr/docs/00/54/97/64/PDF/paclic24_sheiden.pdf

Heiden, S. (2018). Annotation-based Digital Text Corpora Analysis within the TXM Platform. In S. Bolasco, et al. (dirs).. *Proceedings of the 14th JADT'18,* Roma, UniversItalia, pp. 367-374.

Hunston, S. (2002). Corpora in Applied Linguistic. Cambridge: Cambridge University Press.

Kontonatsios, G. (2015). Automatic Compilation of Bilingual Terminologies from Comparable Corpora. Manchester, UK, The University of Manchester, [Thesis].

McEnery, A. (2003). Corpus Linguistics. In R. Mitkov (Ed.) *Oxford Handbook of Computational Linguistics*. Oxford: Oxford University Press, pp. 448-63.

McEnery, T. and Xiao, R. (2007). Parallel and Comparable Corpora: What is Happening?. In Gunilla A. & M. Rogers (Eds.), *Incorporating Corpora: The Linguist and the Translator.* Bristol, Blue Ridge, pp. 18-31. https://doi.org/10.21832/9781853599873-005

Narrog, H. (2016). The Expression of Non-epistemic Modal Categories. In J. Nuyts & J. van der Auwera (Eds.), *The Oxford Handbook of Modality and Mood.* Oxford University Press, Oxford, pp. 89–116.

Nuyts, J. (2005). The Modal Confusion: On Terminology and the Concepts behind it. In A. Klinge et al. (Eds), *Modality. Studies in Form and Function*, Equinox Publishing, pp. 5–38.

Nuyts. J. (2016). Analyses of the Modal Meanings. In J. Nuyts & J. van der Auwera (Eds.), *The Oxford Handbook of Modality and Mood.* Oxford University Press, Oxford, pp. 31–49.

Palmer, F. R. (2001). *Mood and Modality* (2nd ed.). Cambridge University Press.

Paveau, M.-A. (2013). Genre de discours et technologie discursive. In *Pratiques* 157-157, pp. 7-30. DOI: https://doi.org/10.4000/pratiques.3533

Pincemin, B. & Rastier, F. (1999). Des genres à l'intertexte. In *Cahiers de praxématique* 33, pp. 83-111. DOI: https://doi.org/10.4000/praxematique.1974

Sinclair, J. (1996). Preliminary Recommendations on Corpus Typology. In *Rap. tech.*, EAGLES (*Expert Advisory Group on Language Engineering Standards*), CEE.

Talvensaari, T., Laurikkala, J., Järvelin, K., Juhola, M. and Keskustalo, H. (2007). Creating and Exploiting a Comparable Corpus in Cross-language Information Retrieval. ACM (Association for Computing Machinery) Trans. Inf. Syst. [online]. https://doi.org/10.1145/1198296.1198300

Zufferey, S. (2020). Introduction to Corpus Linguistics. John Wiley & Sons.

8. Language Resource References

CLARIN (2021). Virtual Language Observatory. https://vlo.clarin.eu

Proceedings of the 15th Workshop on Building and Using Comparable Corpora (BUCC 2022) @LREC2022 , pages 61–66
Marseille, June 25, 2022
© European Language Resources Association (ELRA), licensed under CC-BY-NC

Fusion of linguistic, neural and sentence-transformer features for improved term alignment

Andraž Repar[1], Boshko Koloski[1], Matej Ulčar[2], Senja Pollak[1]
[1]Jožef Stefan Institute, Jožef Stefan International Postgraduate School
Jamova cesta 39, Ljubljana, Slovenia
[2]Faculty of Computer and Information Science, University of Ljubljana
Večna pot 113, Ljubljana, Slovenia
{andraz.repar,boshko.koloski,senja.pollak}@ijs.si, matej.ulcar@fri.uni-lj.si

Abstract

Crosslingual terminology alignment task has many practical applications. In this work, we propose an aligning method for the shared task of the 15th Workshop on Building and Using Comparable Corpora. Our method combines several different approaches into one cohesive machine learning model, based on SVM. From shared-task specific and external sources, we crafted four types of features: cognate-based, dictionary-based, embedding-based, and combined features, which combine aspects of the other three types. We added a post-processing re-scoring method, which reduces the effect of hubness, where some terms are nearest neighbours of many other terms. We achieved the average precision score of 0.833 on the English-French training set of the shared task.

Keywords: term alignment, cognates, embeddings, sentence-transformers

1. Introduction

Having the ability to align concepts between languages can provide significant benefits in many practical applications, such as aligning terms between languages in bilingual terminology, aligning keywords in news industry or using aligned concepts as seed data for other NLP tasks like multilingual vector space alignment.

In this paper, we present the experiments and their results on the data provided in the bilingual term alignment in comparable specialized corpora shared task organized as part of the 15th Workshop on Building and Using Comparable Corpora (the BUCC workshop). Given a pair of comparable corpora in two languages and a pair of term lists where terms originate in the two corpora, participants were required to produce lists of term pair candidates ranked by their alignment probability (i.e. terms closer to the top are more likely to be true alignments).

Our method involves a machine learning approach based on our work in (Repar et al., 2019) and (Repar et al., 2021) with additional improvements. Our system uses several external resources detailed in Section 3, all of which are publicly available online.

This paper is organized as follows: Section 1 introduces the topic, Section 2 provides the related work, Section 3 describes the methodology, Section 4 contains the results and Section 5 the conclusion.

2. Related work

Initial attempts at bilingual terminology extraction involved parallel input data (Kupiec, 1993; Daille et al., 1994; Gaussier, 1998), and the interest of the community continued until today. However, most parallel corpora are owned by private companies[1], such as language service providers, who consider them to be their intellectual property and are reluctant to share them publicly. For this reason (and in particular for language pairs not involving English) considerable efforts have also been invested into researching bilingual terminology extraction from comparable corpora (Fung and Yee, 1998; Rapp, 1999; Chiao and Zweigenbaum, 2002; Cao and Li, 2002; Daille and Morin, 2005; Morin et al., 2008; Vintar, 2010; Bouamor et al., 2013a; Bouamor et al., 2013b; Hazem and Morin, 2016; Hazem and Morin, 2017).

The approach designed by Aker et al. (2013) and replicated and adapted in Repar et al. (2019) served as the basis of our work. It was developed to align terminology between languages with the help of parallel corpora using machine-learning techniques. They use terms from the Eurovoc (Steinberger et al., 2002) thesaurus and train an SVM binary classifier (Joachims, 2002) (with a linear kernel and the trade-off between training error and margin parameter c = 10). The task of bilingual alignment is treated as a binary classification - each term from the source language S is paired with each term from the target language T and the classifier then decides whether the aligned pair is correct or incorrect. Aker et al. (2013) run their experiments on the 21 official EU languages covered by Eurovoc with English always being the source language (20 language pairs altogether). They evaluate the performance on a held-out term pair list from Eurovoc using recall, precision and F-measure for all 21 languages. Next, they

[1]However, some publicly available parallel corpora do exist. A good overview can be found at the OPUS web portal (Tiedemann, 2012).

propose an experimental setting for a simulation of a real-world scenario where they collect English-German comparable corpora of two domains (IT, automotive) from Wikipedia, perform monolingual term extraction using the system by Pinnis et al. (2012) followed by the bilingual alignment procedure described above and manually evaluate the results (using two evaluators). They report excellent performance on the held-out term list with many language pairs reaching 100% precision and the lowest recall being 65%. For Slovenian, which is of our main interest, the reported results were excellent with perfect or nearly perfect precision and good recall. The reported results of the manual evaluation phase were also good, with two evaluators agreeing that at least 81% of the extracted term pairs in the IT domain and at least 60% of the extracted term pairs in the automotive domain can be considered exact translations. Repar et al. (2019) tried to reproduce their approach and after initially having little success they were at the end able to achieve comparable results with precision exceeding 90% and recall over 50%.

Despite the problem of bilingual term alignment lending itself well to the binary classification task, there have been relatively few approaches utilizing machine learning. Similar to Aker et al. (2013), Baldwin and Tanaka (2004) generate corpus-based, dictionary-based and translation-based features and train an SVM classifier to rank the translation candidates. Note that they only focus on multi-word noun phrases (noun + noun). A similar approach, again focusing on noun phrases, is also described by Cao and Li (2002). Finally, Nassirudin and Purwarianti (2015) also reimplement Aker et al. (2013) for the Indonesian-Japanese language pair and further expand it with additional statistical features.

3. Methodology

Initial experiments were performed with cross-lingual embeddings (see Section 3.1) and sentence transformers (see Section 3.2). However, the results were lower than expected, which is why we adapted an approach described in Repar et al. (2021) by adding additional features based on the cross-lingual embedding and sentence transformer experiments.

3.1. Cross-lingual aligned embeddings

We used fastText Bojanowski et al. (2017) word embeddings for both involved languages. We constructed a bilingual English-French dictionary from Wiktionary entries, using the wikt2dict tool Acs (2014). The extracted dictionary has 204 341 entries. For the purpose of embedding alignment, we filtered it to keep only single-word entries, i.e. those that have a single word in both languages. After the filtering, we had 129 912 entries, of which 24 923 have an identical word in both languages (e.g. place names or chemicals) There's an average of 1.55 English translations for each French word, and 1.56 French translations for each English word. 23.4% of English words have multiple French translations, while 24.3% of French words have multiple English translations.

We then aligned the French and English word embeddings into a common vector space in a supervised manner, utilizing the bilingual dictionary. We used Vecmap Artetxe et al. (2018) tool, which aligns the vectors using the Moore-Penrose pseudo-inverse, which minimizes the sum of squared Euclidean distances. We extracted one vector for each term in each language. For multi-word terms we averaged the word vectors of all the words the term is composed of. Finally we use the cosine similarity score to find the most similar terms in language 1 for each term in language 2, and vice-versa. Using this approach, we achieve an average precision of 0.496 (for details, see Table 2).

3.2. Sentence-transformers features

We used the Sentence-Transformers Reimers and Gurevych (2019) model to embed the terms of the both languages. We utilized the implementations of *c19 python library* (Koloski et al., 2021) to obtain the embeddings [2]. The sentence-transformer architecture is designed to solve the task of sentence similarity, it leverages BERT tokens and via pooling it creates sentence-embeddings. The BERT Devlin et al. (2018) model uses tokens as input to it's transformer architecture, the BERT-tokenizer tokenizes the words in sub-words. We consider using the sentence-transformers because of the sub-word information that is taken into account while learning the model. We feed the model with single or multi-word terms as "sentences" and obtain the sentence-embedding.

3.2.1. Terms as sentences evaluation methodology

For each term in each language respectively we obtain the sentence-embeddings. Next, for each term in English we rank all of the French terms with regards of cosine-similarity.

We consider using five different Language Models:

- XLM (Lample and Conneau, 2019)
- DistilBERT (Sanh et al., 2019)
- All-MPNet (Song et al., 2020)
- MiniLM (Wang et al., 2020)
- Roberta-Large (Liu et al., 2019)

The highest average precision of 0.680 among the five models was achieved with the *distilbert-base* model (for details, see Table 2).

3.3. Supervised machine learning approach

Since the results of the individual approaches described in the previous two sections were lower than expected, we further experimented with combining the individual models into a machine learning model. We reused and

[2] `https://github.com/bkoloskl/c19_rep`

adapted an approach described in Repar et al. (2021) by incorporating the cosine similarity values of the cross-lingual and sentence transformer models into features of the machine learning model.

This approach uses Eurovoc (Steinberger et al., 2002) terms, Giza++ dictionaries (generated from the DGT translation memory (Steinberger et al., 2013)) and word similarity information to generate features for an SVM binary classifier (Joachims, 2002) (with the trade-off between training error and margin parameter c = 10). The model is trained on a list of 7181 Eurovoc English-French term pairs as well as an additional 1.4 million incorrect term pairs generated by randomly pairing English and French Eurovoc terms to simulate real-world conditions. In addition to the binary classification, the model also provides confidence scores which are later used to rank aligned candidate pairs.

For each potential candidate pair, we calculate features of the following types:

- Cognate-based features
- Dictionary-based features
- Embedding-based features
- Combined features

As described in Repar et al. (2019) and Repar et al. (2021), cognate-based features take advantage of word similarity between languages (e.g. *democracy* in English and *démocratie* in French) and dictionary-based features are calculated using results of the Giza++ word alignment algorithm. Embedding-based features are calculated using cosine similarity scores described in Sections 3.1 and 3.2. For each model, we produce a list of word pairs with their cosine similarity scores. These scores are then used to generate embedding features by creating 3-tuples[3] of most similar - based on cosine similarity - source-to-target and target-to-source words, such as:

- xénophobie ['xenophobia', '0.744'], ['racism', '0.6797'], ['anti-semitism', '0.654']
- femme ['woman', '0.7896'], ['women', '0.73'], ['female', '0.722']

where the tuple contains the source language word along with their three most likely corresponding words in the target language and their cosine similarities. The 3-tuples of most similar words were used to construct additional features for the machine learning algorithm as indicated in 1. Finally, combined features combine some aspects of the first three feature types.

[3]This number was determined experimentally.

3.4. Post-process re-ordering

In post-processing we altered the confidence scores of some of the term-pairings. For some term x_1 from language 1, we wanted to ensure that the best performing aligned pair is as close to the top of the list as possible. For x_1, a large number of candidate terms from language 2 can have a high confidence score for a matching term and this might negatively affect the final average precision scores as defined in the shared task, since most terms would not have more than 2-3 correct alignments. Another term x_2 from language 1 might have a lower confidence score with every candidate term from language 2 than all the candidates for x_1. That is, there are such $x_1, x_2 \in L_1$, that $S(x_1, y) > \max_{y'}(S(x_2, y')), \forall y \in L_2$, where S is confidence/similarity score and L_1 and L_2 are languages 1 and 2, respectively. We therefore boosted the confidence scores of the top n candidates for each term by a constant c. Based on the performance on the training dataset, we chose the parameters $n = 1$ and $c = 1.0$.

4. Experimental setup

In step one, we trained the model on publicly available data (Eurovoc thesaurus, Giza++ word alignment lists trained on the DGT corpus and embedding and transformer models trained on the data provided within the BUCC shared task). In step two, we evaluated its performance on the term lists provided as part of the training package in the shared task. To do so, we generated all possible term pairs between the English and French term lists, calculated the features described in Table 1, produced predictions using the model trained in step one and evaluated them against the English-French term list provided as part of the shared task training data.

5. Results

We report results in Table 2. Using just individual language models described in Section 3.2, the best average precision (0.680) is achieved with the distilbert-base model. When we used the SVM approach described in Repar et al. (2021) (i.e. the *SVM old*, we reach an average precision of 0.712 and when we add additional features based on sentence transformer models we achieve an average precision of 0.833 (i.e. *SVM new*. The post-process re-ordering parameters *n* and *c* were as indicated in Section 3.4.

6. Conclusion

In this paper, we presented the results of our experiments for the shared task of the 15th Workshop on Building and Using Comparable Corpora. We first attempted to align terms using cross-lingual embedding and sentence transformer models, but the results were less than satisfactory. Next, we reused an existing machine learning approach and added additional features based on the cross-lingual embedding and sentence

Feature	Cat	Description
isFirstWordTranslated	Dict	Checks whether the first word of the source term is a translation of the first word in the target term (based on the Giza++ dictionary)
isLastWordTranslated	Dict	Checks whether the last word of the source term is a translation of the last word in the target term
percentageOfTranslatedWords	Dict	Ratio of source words that have a translation in the target term
percentageOfNotTranslatedWords	Dict	Ratio of source words that do not have a translation in the target term
longestTranslatedUnitInPercentage	Dict	Ratio of the longest contiguous sequence of source words which has a translation in the target term (compared to the source term length)
longestNotTranslatedUnitInPercentage	Dict	Ratio of the longest contiguous sequence of source words which do not have a translation in the target term (compared to the source term length)
Longest Common Subsequence Ratio	Cogn	Measures the longest common non-consecutive sequence of characters between two strings
Longest Common Substring Ratio	Cogn	Measures the longest common consecutive string (LCST) of characters that two strings have in common
Dice similarity	Cogn	2*LCST / (len(source) + len(target))
Needlemann-Wunsch distance	Cogn	LCST / min(len(source), len(target))
isFirstWordCognate	Cogn	A binary feature which returns True if the longest common consecutive string (LCST) of the first words in the source and target terms divided by the length of the longest of the two words is greater than or equal to a threshold value of 0.7 and both words are longer than 3 characters
isLastWordCognate	Cogn	A binary feature which returns True if the longest common consecutive string (LCST) of the last words in the source and target terms divided by the length of longest of the two words is greater than or equal to a threshold value of 0.7 and both words are longer than 3 characters
Normalized Levensthein distance (LD)	Cogn	1 - LD / max(len(source), len(target))
isFirstWordCovered	Comb	A binary feature indicating whether the first word in the source term has a translation or transliteration in the target term
isLastWordCovered	Comb	A binary feature indicating whether the last word in the source term has a translation or transliteration in the target term
percentageOfCoverage	Comb	Returns the percentage of source term words which have a translation or transliteration in the target term
percentageOfNonCoverage	Comb	Returns the percentage of source term words which have neither a translation nor transliteration in the target term
difBetweenCoverageAndNonCoverage	Comb	Returns the difference between the last two features
isFirstWordMatch	Emd	Checks whether the first word of the source term is the most likely translation of the first word in the target term (based on the aligned embeddings)
isLastWordMatch	Emd	Checks whether the last word of the source term is the most likely translation of the last word in the target term (based on the aligned embeddings)
percentageOfFirstMatchWords	Emb	Ratio of source words that have a first match (i.e. first position in the 3-tuple) in the target term
percentageOfNotFirstMatchWords	Emb	Ratio of source words that do not have a first match (i.e. first position in the 3-tuple) in the target term
longestFirstMatchUnitInPercentage	Emb	Ratio of the longest contiguous sequence of source words which has a first match (first position in the 3-tuple) in the target term (compared to the source term length)
longestNotFirstMatchUnitInPercentage	Emb	Ratio of the longest contiguous sequence of source words which do not have a first match (first position in the 3-tuple) in the target term (compared to the source term length)
isFirstWordTopnMatch	Emd	Checks whether the first word of the source term is in the 3-tuple of most likely translations of the first word in the target term (based on the aligned embeddings)
isLastWordTopnMatch	Emd	Checks whether the first word of the source term is not in the 3-tuple of most likely translations of the first word in the target term (based on the aligned embeddings)
percentageOfTopnMatchWords	Emb	Ratio of source words that have a match (i.e. any position in the 3-tuple) in the target term
percentageOfNotTopnMatchWords	Emb	Ratio of source words that do not have a match (i.e. any position in the 3-tuple) in the target term
longestTopnMatchUnitInPercentage	Emb	Ratio of the longest contiguous sequence of source words which has a match (any position in the 3-tuple) in the target term (compared to the source term length)
longestNotTopnMatchUnitInPercentage	Emb	Ratio of the longest contiguous sequence of source words which do not have a match (any position in the 3-tuple) in the target term (compared to the source term length)
isFirstWordCoveredEmbeddings	Comb	A binary feature indicating whether the first word in the source term has a match (any position in the 3-tuple) or transliteration in the target term
isLastWordCoveredEmbeddings	Comb	A binary feature indicating whether the last word in the source term has a match (any position in the 3-tuple) or transliteration in the target term
percentageOfCoverageEmbeddings	Comb	Returns the percentage of source term words which have a match (any position in the 3-tuple) or transliteration in the target term
percentageOfNonCoverageEmbeddings	Comb	Returns the percentage of source term words which do not have a match (any position in the 3-tuple) or transliteration in the target term
diffBetweenCoverageAnd-NonCoverageEmbeddings	Comb	Returns the difference between the last two features

Table 1: Features used in the experiments. Note that some features are used more than once because they are direction-dependent or used multiple times with different embedding or transformer models.

Model	Average precision
aligned fastText	0.496
distilbert-base	0.680
xlm-r	0.650
all-mpnet	0.616
all-MiniLM	0.621
roberta-large	0.523
SVM old	0.712
SVM new	**0.833**

Table 2: Results

transformer models. Using this model, we achieved the average precision of 0.833. Our experiments show that careful feature engineering could still produce better results than more novel deep learning approaches.

In terms of future work, there is still room for improvement which could be achieved by generating additional features using other transformer or embedding models. The system is also quite resource intensive — model training and prediction on the BUCC dataset took more than 24 hours. Finally, there is also room for a more systematic approach to the postprocess re-ranking step.

7. Acknowledgements

This work was supported by the Slovenian Research Agency (ARRS) grants for the core programme Knowledge technologies (P2-0103), as well as the European Union's Horizon 2020 research and innovation programme under grant agreement No 825153, project EMBEDDIA (Cross-Lingual Embeddings for Less-Represented Languages in European News Media).

8. Bibliographical References

Acs, J. (2014). Pivot-based multilingual dictionary building using Wiktionary. In *Proceedings of the Ninth International Conference on Language Resources and Evaluation LREC*.

Aker, A., Paramita, M., and Gaizauskas, R. (2013). Extracting bilingual terminologies from comparable corpora. In *Proceedings of the 51st Annual Meeting of the Association for Computational Linguistics (Volume 1: Long Papers)*, volume 1, pages 402–411.

Artetxe, M., Labaka, G., and Agirre, E. (2018). Generalizing and improving bilingual word embedding mappings with a multi-step framework of linear transformations. In *Thirty-Second AAAI Conference on Artificial Intelligence*.

Baldwin, T. and Tanaka, T. (2004). Translation by machine of complex nominals: Getting it right. In

Proceedings of the Workshop on Multiword Expressions: Integrating Processing, pages 24–31.

Bojanowski, P., Grave, E., Joulin, A., and Mikolov, T. (2017). Enriching word vectors with subword information. *Transactions of the Association for Computational Linguistics*, 5:135–146.

Bouamor, D., Popescu, A., Semmar, N., and Zweigenbaum, P. (2013a). Building specialized bilingual lexicons using large scale background knowledge. In *Proceedings of the 2013 Conference on Empirical Methods in Natural Language Processing*, pages 479–489, Seattle, Washington, USA, October. Association for Computational Linguistics.

Bouamor, D., Semmar, N., and Zweigenbaum, P. (2013b). Context vector disambiguation for bilingual lexicon extraction from comparable corpora. In *Proceedings of the 51st Annual Meeting of the Association for Computational Linguistics (Volume 2: Short Papers)*, pages 759–764.

Cao, Y. and Li, H. (2002). Base noun phrase translation using web data and the EM algorithm. In *Proceedings of the 19th International Conference on Computational Linguistics - Volume 1*, pages 1–7.

Chiao, Y.-C. and Zweigenbaum, P. (2002). Looking for candidate translational equivalents in specialized, comparable corpora. In *Proceedings of the 19th International Conference on Computational Linguistics - Volume 2*, pages 1–5.

Daille, B. and Morin, E. (2005). French-English terminology extraction from comparable corpora. In *Natural Language Processing – IJCNLP 2005*, pages 707–718.

Daille, B., Gaussier, E., and Langé, J.-M. (1994). Towards automatic extraction of monolingual and bilingual terminology. In *Proceedings of the 15th Conference on Computational Linguistics - Volume 1*, pages 515–521.

Devlin, J., Chang, M.-W., Lee, K., and Toutanova, K. (2018). Bert: Pre-training of deep bidirectional transformers for language understanding. *arXiv preprint arXiv:1810.04805*.

Fung, P. and Yee, L. Y. (1998). An IR approach for translating new words from nonparallel, comparable texts. In *Proceedings of the 17th International Conference on Computational Linguistics - Volume 1*, pages 414–420.

Gaussier, E. (1998). Flow network models for word alignment and terminology extraction from bilingual corpora. In *Proceedings of the 17th International Conference on Computational Linguistics - Volume 1*, pages 444–450.

Hazem, A. and Morin, E. (2016). Efficient data selection for bilingual terminology extraction from comparable corpora. In *Proceedings of COLING 2016, the 26th International Conference on Computational Linguistics: Technical Papers*, pages 3401–3411.

Hazem, A. and Morin, E. (2017). Bilingual word embeddings for bilingual terminology extraction from specialized comparable corpora. In *Proceedings of the 8th International Joint Conference on Natural Language Processing (Volume 1: Long Papers)*, pages 685–693.

Joachims, T. (2002). *Learning to classify text using support vector machines: Methods, theory and algorithms*. Kluwer Academic Publishers.

Koloski, B., Stepišnik-Perdih, T., Pollak, S., and Škrlj, B. (2021). Identification of covid-19 related fake news via neural stacking. In Tanmoy Chakraborty, et al., editors, *Combating Online Hostile Posts in Regional Languages during Emergency Situation*, pages 177–188, Cham. Springer International Publishing.

Kupiec, J. (1993). An algorithm for finding noun phrase correspondences in bilingual corpora. In *Proceedings of the 31st annual meeting on Association for Computational Linguistics*, pages 17–22.

Lample, G. and Conneau, A. (2019). Cross-lingual language model pretraining.

Liu, Y., Ott, M., Goyal, N., Du, J., Joshi, M., Chen, D., Levy, O., Lewis, M., Zettlemoyer, L., and Stoyanov, V. (2019). Roberta: A robustly optimized BERT pretraining approach. *CoRR*, abs/1907.11692.

Morin, E., Daille, B., Takeuchi, K., and Kageura, K. (2008). Brains, not brawn: The use of smart comparable corpora in bilingual terminology mining. *ACM Trans. Speech Lang. Process.*, 7(1):1:1–1:23, October.

Nassirudin, M. and Purwarianti, A. (2015). Indonesian-Japanese term extraction from bilingual corpora using machine learning. In *Advanced Computer Science and Information Systems (ICACSIS), 2015 International Conference on*, pages 111–116.

Pinnis, M., Ljubešić, N., Stefanescu, D., Skadina, I., Tadić, M., and Gornostaya, T. (2012). Term extraction, tagging, and mapping tools for under-resourced languages. In *Proceedings of the 10th Conference on Terminology and Knowledge Engineering (TKE 2012), June*, pages 20–21.

Rapp, R. (1999). Automatic identification of word translations from unrelated english and german corpora. In *Proceedings of the 37th Annual Meeting of the Association for Computational Linguistics on Computational Linguistics*, pages 519–526.

Reimers, N. and Gurevych, I. (2019). Sentence-bert: Sentence embeddings using siamese bert-networks. *CoRR*, abs/1908.10084.

Repar, A., Martinc, M., and Pollak, S. (2019). Reproduction, replication, analysis and adaptation of a term alignment approach. *Language Resources and Evaluation*, pages 1–34.

Repar, A., Martinc, M., Ulčar, M., and Pollak, S. (2021). Word-embedding based bilingual terminology alignment. *Electronic lexicography in the 21st century (eLex 2021) Post-editing lexicography*, page 98.

Sanh, V., Debut, L., Chaumond, J., and Wolf,

T. (2019). Distilbert, a distilled version of BERT: smaller, faster, cheaper and lighter. *CoRR*, abs/1910.01108.

Song, K., Tan, X., Qin, T., Lu, J., and Liu, T. (2020). Mpnet: Masked and permuted pre-training for language understanding. *CoRR*, abs/2004.09297.

Steinberger, R., Pouliquen, B., and Hagman, J. (2002). Cross-lingual document similarity calculation using the multilingual thesaurus eurovoc. *Computational Linguistics and Intelligent Text Processing*, pages 101–121.

Steinberger, R., Eisele, A., Klocek, S., Pilos, S., and Schlüter, P. (2013). DGT-TM: A freely available translation memory in 22 languages. In *Proceedings of the 8th international conference on Language Resources and Evaluation (LREC'2012).*

Tiedemann, J. (2012). Parallel data, tools and interfaces in opus. In Nicoletta Calzolari (Conference Chair), et al., editors, *Proceedings of the Eight International Conference on Language Resources and Evaluation (LREC'12)*, Istanbul, Turkey, may. European Language Resources Association (ELRA).

Vintar, Š. (2010). Bilingual term recognition revisited: The bag-of-equivalents term alignment approach and its evaluation. *Terminology. International Journal of Theoretical and Applied Issues in Specialized Communication*, 16(2):141–158.

Wang, W., Wei, F., Dong, L., Bao, H., Yang, N., and Zhou, M. (2020). Minilm: Deep self-attention distillation for task-agnostic compression of pre-trained transformers. In H. Larochelle, et al., editors, *Advances in Neural Information Processing Systems*, volume 33, pages 5776–5788. Curran Associates, Inc.

9. Language Resource References

Author Index

Association for Computational Linguistics
209 N. Eighth Street
Stroudsburg, Pennsylvania 18360

ISBN 978-1-7138-6113-3

CURRAN ASSOCIATES INC.
proceedings.com

International Conference on Ship Conversion, Repair & Maintenance 2021

Online
26 January 2021

The Royal Institution of
Naval Architects